What Really Happened on October 5, 1892

An Attempt at an Accurate Account of the Dalton Gang and Coffeyville

Lue Diver Barndollar

Roots & Branches

Denton, Texas

Roots & Branches
An imprint of AWOC.COM Publishing
P.O. Box 2819
Denton, TX 76202

Manufactured in the United States of America.

ISBN: 978-1-62016-110-4 Paperback
ISBN: 978-1-62016-111-1 Ebook

Table of Contents

List of Figures 4

Foreword to the 2014 Reprint 5

Foreword 7

Preface 9

Chapter 1: The Area 14

Chapter 2: The Family 23

Chapter 3: The Lawmen 29

Chapter 4: The Outlaws 36

Chapter 5: The Approach 46

Chapter 6: The Raid 54

Chapter 7: The Alley 70

Chapter 8: The Aftermath 74

Afterword 104

Bibliography 107

List of Figures

Figure 1.1. Coffeyville in 1871

Figure 1.2. The Plaza Block in 1881

Figure 1.3. The East Side of Union in 1885

Figure 1.4. The West Side of Walnut in 1888

Figure 1.5. The West Side of Walnut in 1892

Figure 1.6. Walnut Street and the Plaza Block in 1895

Figure 5.1. Map of Plaza Area in 1892

Figure 5.2. Death Alley Fence where Outlaws tied their Horses

Figure 5.3. City Jail on South Side of Alley

Figure 5.4. The East Side of Walnut

Figure 5.5. Rock found near Allin's Hill

Figure 6.1. The Condon Bank in 1892

Figure 6.2. Cubine's Boot and Shoe Shop

Figure 6.3. Doorframe of the Condon Vault Entrance

Figure 6.4. The First National Bank Safe

Figure 8.1. Instruments belonging to Dr. W. H. Wells

Figure 8.2. Death Alley after the Raid

Figure 8.3. A Closer View of Death Alley

Figure 8.4. The Dalton Gang: Four Dead, One Alive

Figure 8.5. Bob's Boot Gun and the Burial Records

Figure 8.6. Marshall Connelly's Gun with Mementoes

Figure 8.7. Burlap Money Sack with Gun Baldwin Carried

Figure 8.8. Kloehr's Picture, Medal, Badge, and Gun

Figure 8.9. A Close-up of the Medal

Figure 8.10. Bob's Saddle with Grat's Rifle

Figure 8.11. Bob's Pearl-Handled Revolver with Cartridge Belt
    and Oil Can

Figure 8.12. Bob's Vest-Pocket .38 Caliber British Bulldog

Figure 8.13. Judge McCue's Desk, Grat's Rifle, and Trial Docket

Figure 8.14. Emmett's Six-Shooter with Warrant and Cartridge Belt

Figure 8.15. Bill Power's Revolver

Figure 8.16. Bullet Holes in Condon Windows

Figure 8.17. Cartridge Belt showing Damaged Cartridge

Foreword to the 2014 Reprint

It has been twenty-some years since the Coffeyville Historical Society published this book to commemorate the hundredth anniversary of the Dalton Raid in Coffeyville. The goal of the original publication was to compile as much information as possible about the deadly raid on October 5, 1892. Local photographer Tackett had taken pictures immediately after the shooting stopped, so his photographs were of immeasurable value in verifying the happenings of that terrible day. Firsthand accounts, including Elliott's newspaper article published two days after the raid, were complemented in this book both by Tackett's pictures and by many accounts written long after the raid took place. A few of the latter offered various creative explanations and occurrences that cannot be verified. Others simply repeated inaccuracies which, over time, had been listed as facts.

Although reprinted by the Coffeyville Historical Society in 2001, the book has been generally unavailable for some years, except for those resold on Amazon.com and through other venues. Prices quoted to the Society for additional reprints after 2001 were simply more than the entity's budget would allow.

However, since 2001, the world of publishing and marketing has changed significantly. It is hoped that this current reprint in both print and electronic formats will make the story of Coffeyville and the Daltons more accessible to interested readers.

The basic outline of that October day in 1892 has *not* changed. Four outlaws died and the fifth was severely wounded in an attempt to rob Coffeyville's two banks. Four Coffeyville citizens died and three were wounded as they defended their town. These—and the other Defenders—are the heroes of the event. They demonstrated courage and self-reliance as they sought to protect their town. They did what needed to be done.

History offers many lessons from which we can profit today. Willa Cather, a Nebraska author who achieved recognition for her novels of frontier life on the Great Plains, wrote in her novel *Oh, Pioneers:* "The history of every country begins in the heart of a man or a woman." The Defenders of Coffeyville—on that infamous day in 1892—proved they had the heart to do what had to be done—and thus wrote a new chapter in our country's history.

—Lue Diver Barndollar

Foreword

This book has been produced in 1992 as a joint effort between the Coffeyville Historical Society and the Dalton Centennial Committee.

Much misinformation has appeared, both in print and on film over the past century, concerning the raid on Coffeyville's banks. It was felt that due to the interest in the raid, it would be fitting to produce as accurate a compilation as possible of the facts about the people and events involved. The resulting account is intended as a memorial to those citizens killed and injured in the raid and to their families.

Our sincere thanks and appreciation go to Mrs. Lue Barndollar for the many hours of research and extraction of information from many different published accounts of the Dalton family and the raid. She has attempted to convey as accurate an account as possible using information based on primary source material and original documents presented in previous publications.

Lue Diver Barndollar is an English instructor and division chair at Coffeyville Community College. Her parents—who were raised in Iola and Neosho Falls, Kansas—came to Coffeyville in 1936. Her maternal grandfather, Lew Wallace Duncan, wrote both the *History of Montgomery County, Kansas* (1903) and the *History of Allen and Woodson Counties* (1901). Her husband's grandfather, James Judson Barndollar, settled in Coffeyville in 1871 and established the Barndollar Brothers store which was on the plaza at the time of the Dalton raid.

We also want to thank the J.M. Davis Gun Museum of Claremore, Oklahoma for allowing us to photograph Emmett Dalton's and Bill Power's revolvers. Thanks also to Mr. John Neale for the opportunity to photograph one of Bob Dalton's revolvers. The color photography was done by Mr. Floyd Graham of Coffeyville. The cover illustration was provided by Don Sprague. A Coffeyville native and talented artist, Sprague specializes in historical paintings. He also has painted a series of murals on Coffeyville buildings depicting the town's history. Acknowledgement is also due to Mrs. Phyllis Schenk for many hours of assistance in the composition of this book for printing. Our appreciation also goes to the numerous other people who have contributed time and effort to this publication.

Gary Misch, President
Coffeyville Historical Society

Preface

August 1992

The romance which surrounds the Old West—the romance of the self-sufficient individual, the romance of the cowboy and the Indian, the romance of the lawman and the desperado—is perhaps nowhere else so evident as in the story of the Dalton gang raid in Coffeyville, Kansas, on October 5th of 1892, one hundred years ago.

One hundred years is a long time. The city of Coffeyville has experienced many history-making occasions which threatened the life and limb of some of its citizenry during the period since 1892: the 1917 tornado, the 1943 flood, the 1944 explosion at the Co-op Refinery, the 1954 fire which destroyed the South Coffeyville facilities of Funk Aircraft, the 1980 Memorial Auditorium fire, and the 1983 light plant explosion.

None of these historic occurrences, neither the longest ago nor the most recent, has become the stuff of legend. The explosion at the Refinery during World War II, in which eleven died, was rumored to be sabotage; the Memorial Hall fire was arson, yet no one has written a book about or made a movie of either of these events. Maybe the answer is that these and similar events have occurred elsewhere. But a hundred years ago Coffeyville experienced one historic event which has never occurred anywhere else. A gunfight occasioned by the attempt to rob two banks at the same time caused the death of four citizens, the death of four outlaws, and wounds to four others: the Dalton raid on Coffeyville.

Writing about an 1892 event in 1992 presents the problem of the accuracy of existing records. Eyewitnesses to the Dalton raid are no longer living, and the records which exist from eyewitness or second-hand eyewitness accounts seldom agree. This issue is not unique to the story of the Dalton raid; even the Gospels of Matthew, Mark, Luke, and John do not tell exactly the same story. The passing of time affects one's memory. Eyewitness accounts written soon after an event seem more reliable than those written after the passing of years has had a chance to put moth holes in the curtain that divides what one experienced and witnessed from what one heard about from others. Memoirs, written long after the fact, are always interesting but not always trustworthy.

The data from history books sometimes vary from the eyewitness accounts and from the information from memoirs. Then, in addition to eyewitness accounts, memoirs, and actual histories, library shelves are filled with so-called history books, which often take great liberties with facts, even inventing new characters and new motives. Other possible sources of information are historical novels, which seek to make the details of history into best sellers and make no distinction between fact and fiction.

This information problem reared its head as I attempted to write as accurate a version as possible of the story of the Dalton gang and Coffeyville. I quickly discovered that the tale has many versions with variations ranging from the minute to the gigantic.

In general I have trusted eyewitness accounts written soon after the event, believing their inconsistencies represented different points of view rather than efforts to manipulate the evidence. The variations I found in actual history books were minor. When memoirs and so-called histories (which often seemed to present an entirely different story) varied from what I call the mainstream of the story, my suspicions were aroused. Novels I have always enjoyed and respected for what they are: novels. As works of fiction, they presented no research problem.

In compiling the available information, I have tried to point out both some of the inconsistencies and some of the exaggerations and untruths which were created to make a good story better.

One exception exists to my policy regarding eyewitness accounts. Emmett Dalton's books, *When the Daltons Rode* and *Beyond the Law*, cannot be considered reliable. Other researchers who sought to verify the facts found this out long before I did. His relatives knew it too. Emmett's step-granddaughter, Hazel Chapman, told a reporter, "Julia [Emmett's wife] brought Em's book and laid it on my mother's dining room table and they just laughed at it, because it wasn't true." Emmett's family wasn't particularly upset. "There's a lot of myths, but that's what sells books and articles" (Craven 11).

As an example of one of these myths, Chapman used Emmett's story, often reprinted, that her grandmother, Julia Johnson, was Emmett's childhood sweetheart who waited patiently for him to get out of prison so they could marry. In reality, Julia first married Rob Gilstrap, who was murdered in 1889, then Robert Earnest Lewis, who was killed in 1907. According to Chapman, Julia didn't even meet Emmett until after his release from prison in 1908 (Craven 11).

Emmett apparently didn't wait to write his books before altering the facts of the raid. Chapman said Emmett had told her grandmother that his brothers wouldn't let him go with them to the banks. He was just 19, so they made him stay and guard their horses (Craven 12). This tale might be one Emmett convinced himself of while he was in prison, but too many eyewitnesses place Emmett at the robbery scene for this to be the actual case.

The movies which have appeared about the Daltons also have been full of invention. The Daltons were featured in at least one silent film. Then, in 1940, Universal released *When The Daltons Rode*—the most successful of all the Dalton films—and, in 1945, *The Daltons Ride Again*. In 1957 United Artists released *The Dalton Girls*. Two made-for-television movies featuring the Daltons were *The Last Day*, in 1975, and *The Last Ride of the Dalton Gang*, in 1979. None of these movies could be acclaimed for accuracy (Huff "Movies" 13).

At least two books have been written about the Daltons that do not claim to be factual. *The Sixth Rider: a Novel of the Dalton Gang*, by Max McCoy, is admittedly a fictional account. McCoy stated, "It's meant for entertainment" (Pippenger 14). Another book about the Daltons which admits to being a novel is *The Desperadoes*, written by Ron Hansen.

I don't presume to state that all the errors and untruths written about the Daltons were set down deliberately. Many writers were simply repeating details they had read in other sources or had heard from contemporaries or eyewitnesses. Every detail about the Dalton gang was newsworthy. In an era without radio and television, news circulated either on paper or from mouth to mouth. Coffeyville's newspaper, *The Journal,* was at that time a weekly paper and not widely available, so Dalton tales containing only an acorn of truth sometimes grew into huge oaks.

I make no claim for infallibility. I have simply sought to present the most accurate view of the Daltons and the raid possible, given the sources and the time at my disposal. Although my account undoubtedly contains errors, I am certain that it is more reputable than some of its predecessors.

I have appreciated the help of Karyl Buffington and other staff at the Coffeyville Public Library as I dug away at microfilm and other sources. Although I have cited and commented on various sources throughout the text, the research of one particular author deserves mention here. Nancy Samuelson's works present what is the closest to a true history of the Daltons. Her two studies have been immensely interesting and tremendously helpful.

I must thank Cindy Price of the Coffeyville Convention and Visitors' Bureau and Gary Misch of the Coffeyville Historical Society for their help—and for suggesting I undertake this research. As in any other endeavor, the person who actually does the digging benefits most of all.

My greatest vote of thanks goes to my husband, who has proofread, commented, and listened as I excitedly recounted some newly-uncovered tidbit. He and I both have gained an even greater appreciation for our hometown and its history than we had previously. We are glad that we have had the opportunity to be raised—and to raise our children—in Coffeyville, Kansas. Coffeyville is a town whose citizens have met and dealt with adversity many times, a town where citizens from all walks of life do whatever is necessary to protect their town and make it a better place to live, a town where the citizenry rose to the occasion during the Dalton raid on October 5, 1892.

Chapter 1: The Area

Anna E. Arnold's work, *A History of Kansas*, serves as the principal source for this chapter. Most of the following information about the area comes from her work. Other sources used are indicated in the text.

To understand the events of the Dalton raid on Coffeyville that morning in October of 1892, we need to understand something of the history of the area.

From the time of the Louisiana Purchase in 1803, the area that would eventually be called Kansas was used primarily as a path to the west by explorers, traders, settlers, and gold seekers. Since the white man did not yet want to settle there, the area remained home to Indians. The tribes who lived in eastern Kansas were the Kanza and the Osage. The Kanza lived north of the Kansas River (now called the Kaw) and the Osage south of it (18, 37).

In 1825 the U. S. government made treaties with both the Kanza and the Osage. These treaties restricted the two tribes to a small portion of their original territories. In return the government was to supply the Indians with livestock and implements with which to farm and with blacksmithing and agricultural instruction. The area of southeast Kansas that was later to be settled as Coffeyville was a part of the territory left to the Osage in their 1825 treaty, though the government retained the right to use trails through their lands (Howes 3).

The areas of Kansas which were opened by these 1825 treaties were soon filled with groups of other Indian tribes. These tribes moved in because of an 1830 act under which the government took their lands in the eastern part of the U. S. and gave them certain lands in areas which included eastern Kansas (41).

During the years between 1803 and 1854, the only white men who settled in eastern Kansas were fur trappers and traders, missionaries, and soldiers. As white settlers began to see the desirability of the lands in eastern Kansas, the government (certainly not known for its just treatment of the Indian) began moving Indians again in 1854, this time transferring the Indians earlier moved to Kansas to Indian Territory. This Indian Territory (I. T.), later to become the state of Oklahoma, was defined as the area south of the Kansas line and north of the Red River (Howes 12-13).

What to do with the Indians was not the government's only problem during the 19th century. The issue of slavery had divided the nation. The balance of power between free and slave state representation in the U. S. Senate had been closely watched since at least 1790. Each side hoped to secure a majority in order to pass favorable legislation. (Because of its greater population, the North had the majority in the House of Representatives.). Therefore free and slave states were admitted alternately to the Union so that a balance was kept between the number of pro-slavery and free-state senators.

The Missouri Compromise of 1820 had stated that Missouri could enter the Union as a slave state, but that all the rest of the territory included in the Louisiana Purchase and north of the southern boundary of Missouri should be free forever. However, by the 1850s the Missouri Compromise was outdated. The relations between North and South were even more strained than they had been in 1820. When Congress passed the Kansas-Nebraska Bill in 1854, organizing the two territories, the act decreed that each territory should have popular sovereignty, that is, be able to decide for itself whether to become slave or free (54).

The Southern states believed that Nebraska would come into the Union as a free state; therefore they were determined that Kansas should come into the Union as a slave state. The vocal strife that had been going on in Congress soon became physical strife in the Kansas Territory, which developed into a war zone. It is from those years after 1854, especially those between 1854 and 1857 that the term "Bleeding Kansas" emerged.

The only state bordering Kansas was Missouri, a slave state, so it was natural that many Southern sympathizers began to settle the new Kansas Territory. Those settlers who wanted to claim land had to build houses and use the land as homes for a certain period of time. Many of the Missouri settlers met these requirements; others did not. Some laid out the shape of a house or posted notices, then returned to Missouri to live (58).

The Northern states had as a part of their population many foreign immigrants, laborers, small farmers, and small shopkeepers. It wasn't too difficult to persuade some of those individuals to go settle in Kansas to help keep it a free state. The Southern states, populated more with plantation owners and slaves, didn't find it so easy to enlist people to go settle in Kansas. Be that as it may, both sides did begin lining up people to become Kansas settlers. The New England Emigrant Aid Society and others sent groups of anti-slavery settlers, and organizations in the South, such as the Alabama Society, sent pro-slavery settlers to Kansas (Howes 30).

The first party of free-staters settled in the area now known as Lawrence. It soon became the town most hated by the pro-slavery people (64). The establishment of both pro-slavery and free-state territorial governments brought on bloodshed. Both pro-slavery and free-state supporters (the later called Jayhawkers) chose to take the law into their own hands. They tried to starve or frighten each other out of the Territory (75).

A number of minor skirmishes occurred before the pro-slavery leaders sacked Lawrence on May 21, 1856, doing a tremendous amount of damage, but killing no one (77-78). A small group of free-staters led by John Brown then made a raid on a pro-slavery settlement near Pottawatomie Creek and killed five settlers (79). These murders brought about additional violent acts on both sides. Arnold included the following quote from Territorial Governor John W. Geary, who arrived in 1856:

> I reached Kansas ... in the most gloomy hour of her history. Desolation and ruin reigned on every hand; homes and firesides were deserted; the smoke of burning dwellings darkened the atmosphere; women and children, driven from their habitations, wandered over the prairies and among the woodlands, or sought refuge even among the Indian tribes. The highways were infested with numerous predatory bands, and the towns were fortified and garrisoned by armies of conflicting partisans, each excited almost to frenzy, and determined upon mutual extermination. Such was, without exaggeration, the condition of the Territory at the period of my arrival. (83)

This is the era during which Lewis and Adeline Dalton began raising their family. By the time Governor Geary arrived in 1856, four of their children had already been born. Five more would be born to them before the eastern Kansas/western Missouri border where they lived would no longer be a no-man's land.

On January 29th in 1861—the year Grat Dalton was born—Kansas finally entered the Union as the 34th state, a free-state. Shortly before this, several of the Southern states seceded from the Union. The Civil War began on April 12, 1861, only three months later (103).

One of the worst features of the war for the new state of Kansas was the continuing border trouble. Groups, including Quantrill's, plundered and destroyed property. The Quantrill raid on Lawrence, on August 21, 1863, was the murderous climax. With a band of 450 border ruffians, Quantrill burned and looted Lawrence, killing about 150 citizens and wounding untold numbers of others. The property loss in Lawrence was later estimated at between one and two million dollars (104-05).

The end of the Civil War in April 1865 at last gave the people of Kansas an opportunity to begin more normal activities. Hundreds of new settlers entered the state, some hoping to farm, some hoping to start businesses. This influx of newcomers was true in southeast Kansas just as it was for the rest of the state.

In the late 1860s Colonel John A. Coffey established a trading post on what is now South Walnut Street in Coffeyville. He built this post in order to trade with the Black Dog band of the Osage. In August of 1869—the year Bob Dalton was born—Colonel Coffey and others laid out the town of Coffeyville around the trading post. By 1871 the Leavenworth, Lawrence, and Galveston railroad (later to become the Santa Fe) had rails reaching almost to the Kansas/Indian Territory border. The railroad company accordingly laid out a townsite just north of Colonel Coffey's "Old Town" of Coffeyville (*Coffeyville at 100* 8).

The town grew rapidly with the coming of the railroad. Herds of cattle were driven to the railhead for shipment. Coffeyville became a cow town. Freight wagons traveled south and west. Saloons and dance houses opened to entertain the cowboys, cattlemen, soldiers, and Indians who filled the town on paydays. The rougher part of the town was known as "Red Hot Street" (*Coffeyville at 100* 11-12).

Figure 1.1. Coffeyville in 1871

Coffeyville also grew in more settled ways. A Catholic church was built in 1870, and a Methodist church was organized that same year. During 1871 the Eldridge House hotel and the Perkins building were erected. The first public school was opened. Senator E. G. Ross, whose 1868 vote had saved President Johnson from being impeached, founded a newspaper in Coffeyville.

Figure 1.2. The Plaza Block in 1881

Hale, Isham and Co, claiming to have "the largest hardware stock in Southeast Kansas" advertised in Ross's paper (*Coffeyville at 100* 15). In 1872 Read Brothers opened their dry goods and clothing store. Additional newspapers were established, the *Coffeyville Journal* in 1875. The banking house of Thomas G. Ayres and Company was created in 1880. Prohibition passed in Kansas that same year, with Coffeyville citizens voting with the majority (*Coffeyville at 100* 11-19).

Such was the town of Coffeyville, Kansas, when the Dalton family arrived. Duncan's *History of Montgomery County*, published in 1903, states that the Daltons settled in the Coffeyville vicinity in 1882 and remained in the area until the opening of Oklahoma in 1889 (33).[1]

Figure 1.3. The East Side of Union in 1885

By 1885 The Ayres banking house was reorganized into the First National Bank of Coffeyville. On July 20th of that year, the buildings on the plaza, including the Perkins building, were completely destroyed by fire. The Condon Bank was established in 1886, with C. T.

Carpenter as the junior partner and C. M. Ball as cashier. (*Coffeyville at 100* 19-21).

Figure 1.4. The West Side of Walnut in 1888

In 1887 the Missouri Pacific railroad came to Coffeyville. That year the fast-growing city claimed a population of over 2,000, making it a city of the Second Class. By 1892 gas drilling was underway. In May the biggest well to date on the Mid-Continent field was brought in. In July a rich gas well was drilled in the center of town. (*Coffeyville at 100* 22-23).

Figure 1.5. The West Side of Walnut in 1892

Figure 1.6. Walnut Street and the Plaza Block in 1895

That was the city of Coffeyville, Kansas, with a population now grown to about 4,000 souls, as October 1892 neared. Hopefully, this brief history of the area has set the scene for what is to follow. First, however, we need some information about the Dalton family.

Notes to Chapter 1: The Area

1   Duncan probably considered Vinita, Indian Territory—about 45 miles from Coffeyville—to be in the vicinity. See Chapter 2 for more information about this date problem.

Chapter 2: The Family

Nancy B. Samuelson's reliable study, *The Dalton Gang Family*, serves as the principal source for this chapter. Most of the following information about the Dalton family comes from this 1989 work. Because of its brevity, individual page numbers are cited only for direct quotes. Other sources used are indicated in the text.

To understand the events of that morning in October of 1892, we need to understand something of Grat, Bob, and Emmett Dalton's family.

The three men were sons of James Lewis Dalton (born February 16, 1826), who had come to Missouri from Kentucky after serving as a fifer in the Second Kentucky Infantry during the Mexican War. At the time of his marriage (March 12, 1851), he had a saloon business at Westport Landing, now a part of Kansas City.[1] His teenage bride, Adeline Lee Younger (born September 5, 1835) was a teetotaler; she eventually convinced him to get out of the saloon business (Samuelson *Story* 30, Preece 13).

Adeline was the daughter of Charles Younger, who had moved to Missouri from Virginia, and Parmelia Dorcus Wilson. Emmett wrote that Adeline's half-brother, Henry Washington Younger, was killed by Jayhawkers in July 1862. His home was later burned and the family turned out in the cold (*When the Daltons Rode* 21). One of Henry's daughters married one of Quantrill's raiders. Four of Henry's sons—Cole, Jim,

John, and Bob—eventually made up the outlaw group known as the Youngers.[2]

Adeline and Lewis had fifteen children. Samuelson lists the names and dates as follows:

> Charles Benjamin (1852-1936)
> Henry Coleman (1853-1920)
> Louis Kossuth (1855-1862)
> Bea Elizabeth (1856—after 1891)—probably
>   nicknamed Lelia
> Littleton Lee (1857-1942)
> Franklin "Frank" (1859-1887)
> Gratten Hanley "Grat" (1861-1892)
> Mason Frakes "Bill" (1863-1894)[3]
> Eva Mae (1867-1939)
> Robert Rennick "Bob" (1869-1892)
> Emmett (1871-1937)
> Leona Randolph (1875-1964)
> Nancy May "Nannie" (1876-1901)
> Hanna Adeline (1878-1878)
> Simon Noel (1878-1928)—twin of Hanna Adeline

Littleton Dalton said the family lived near Independence, Missouri, when he was born in 1857. By 1860 the family had moved west to near Denver, Colorado, but by 1861 they were back in Kansas, near Lawrence. They moved to Liberty, Missouri, later to get away from the fighting (Latta 2, 4, 22). By 1870 the family was in Cass County Missouri, and in 1880 they were in Bates County Missouri. Emmett wrote that Lewis moved his family into what is now northeast Oklahoma in 1882 (*When the Daltons Rode* 25). They squatted near Vinita until moving to Coffeyville in 1886 (Dary 122).[4] Lewis died July 16, 1890, in Montgomery County Kansas. Lewis is said to be buried in Robbins Cemetery near Dearing, Kansas, just west of Coffeyville, though no marker can be found. Adeline died at 92

(January 24, 1925) in Kingfisher, Oklahoma, and is buried there (Samuelson *Story* 30).

Most accounts of the Dalton family mention Lewis's ne'er-do-well habits which relegated the family to poverty.[5] According to Littleton, his mother didn't have a stove for the first twenty years of her marriage; she cooked over a fireplace until 1871 (Latta 13). Lewis Dalton certainly didn't seem interested in farming. Dary said at one time he became a barker in a traveling circus (122). He did love horses. Emmett wrote that, when he was eleven, his father bought a horse that had belonged to Jesse James. It is easy to imagine the excitement created among the Dalton boys when they had the opportunity to ride a horse which had actually belonged to and been ridden by the notorious outlaw (*When the Daltons Rode* 21-22).

Hunting provided other excitement. Littleton said he and the other boys used to shoot "wild turkey, ducks, geese, quail, raccoon, rabbits, possum, bear, deer, and a number of fur-bearing animals." Wild fruits and nuts were abundant. "With a little corn, beans, and bacon, for use in a pinch," the Dalton family managed to eat fairly well (Latta 12).

All accounts agreed that Lewis loved horse trading. He would travel far and wide trading, racing, and betting on horses, spending or losing whatever money came in. Grandfather Younger had left Adeline a colored servant, Aunt Liddy, who had been a nurse to the Dalton children. When Littleton was seven, Lewis sold Aunt Liddy for eight hundred dollars; financing another trip with his horses was more important to him than Adeline's need for help with the eight children they had by that year (Latta 17). It's certain that Lewis Dalton wasn't much of a family man; Adeline had both the responsibility of raising the family and the responsibility of providing for them.

According to Emmett, Adeline was the disciplinarian, administering sound spankings when the children squabbled. Lewis was more easy-going, claiming that his Mexican War experience had made him realize he was not a fighter (*When the Daltons Rode* 17). (Author's note: Lewis wasn't a fighter, and he certainly wasn't a very good father either. Any parent knows it's easier **not** to disciple children.) Latta quoted Littleton as saying his father "never did provide for his family" (22). Lewis wasn't around much to help with things like providing food and discipline, but he definitely stopped by now and then. Adeline and Lewis were married for thirty-nine years. During the first twenty-seven years of their marriage she bore him fifteen children.)[6]

Thirteen of the fifteen Dalton children lived to grow up; nine of the thirteen turned out well. Preece says, "It was just one more nail in a good woman's cross" that Grat and the brothers immediately following him started arriving just as the North and South were ready to take up arms (15).

I agree with Samuelson that western Missouri and eastern Kansas were not ideal locations in which to raise children in the 1850s and 1860s. It is clear that Adeline did the best she could, and her family knew it. In none of the published comments of any of her children have I found a word of criticism of their mother.

Though history would come to identify the Daltons with acts on the wrong side of the law, the four of the Dalton offspring who are of special interest to Coffeyville grew up to become lawmen. Their work as lawmen is the subject for the next chapter.

Notes to Chapter 2: The Family

1 Although Littleton Dalton said that his mother was born in 1825 and married his father in 1841, the records Samuelson has

located make it probable that Littleton's memory for dates was off (Latta 9).

2   Thus the outlaws known as the Younger gang were cousins (or half-cousins, to be exact) of the Daltons. The Youngers rode with Frank and Jesse James. John Younger was killed in a gunfight in 1874. Jim, Bob, and Cole Younger were with the Jameses when they attempted to rob the First National Bank at Northfield, MN. Cole was shot eleven times, and Jim was shot five times during the Northfield debacle. The three Youngers surrendered to the law in 1876 and were serving life terms in the Minnesota penitentiary by the time of the Dalton Raid on Coffeyville (McLoughlin 559-60).

There is no evidence to support the idea that the Daltons were related to the James gang, although Burton Rascoe, in his Introduction to *The Dalton Brothers by An Eye Witness*, wrote that the James brothers were "remote blood-kin" of the Daltons (16). During their fifteen years of activity the James gang robbed seven banks, seven trains, and at least three stagecoaches. By the time of the Dalton raid on Coffeyville, the James gang, too, had met its nemesis. Jesse James had been killed near Kansas City in 1882 by one of his own relatives (McLoughlin 252-54).

I could find no evidence either to prove or to disprove the oft-repeated claim that the Dalton raid on Coffeyville was planned as an attempt to outdo the James gang.

3   Horan (149) and others incorrectly stated that Bill's name was William Marion. Littleton said Bill's name was Mason Frakes, and the family called him Mason, though Bill was his nickname outside the family (Latta 22). Samuelson cites census records where he is listed as Mason Frakes.

4   Steele claimed that Lewis Dalton, on his 1887 pension application, wrote that the family moved to the Coffeyville area in 1880 and lived there until 1883. They supposedly lived near Vinita from 1883 to 1887. There is obviously some confusion about just when the family lived in Coffeyville, but it is a fact that Lewis died near Coffeyville in 1890.

5   Emmett was the only source I found who intimated that the Dalton family were not living from hand to mouth. In *When the Daltons Rode*, he wrote their home was filled with "peace, plenty, and content" (23). Everything that Emmett wrote should

be taken with a grain of salt. I don't believe this statement—even with salt.

6 Samuelson, in *The Dalton Gang Story*, writes that the stories about a divorce between Lewis and Adeline were a fabrication (27). However, at least one contemporary account supported the idea that divorce was mentioned. In a 1953 newspaper article Irene Elliott, daughter of David Stewart Elliott, was reported as saying Adeline Dalton had considered divorcing Lewis. Sometime before the Coffeyville raid Miss Elliot had met the Daltons when Mrs. Dalton had come to the Elliott home so that she could consult Mr. Elliott (who was a lawyer as well as the *Journal* editor) about a possible divorce. Several of Mrs. Dalton's family members had come with her to the Elliott residence as moral support ("Too Excited").

Irene Elliott (born 1879) was my husband's first cousin once removed. From 1953 until her death in 1964, I had many conversations with her both about Coffeyville history and about family history. Although the passage of time might have made her memory less accurate, I have never found her in error on any of the family history that I have been able to check through other sources. Because of Miss Elliott's testimony—and because of what I have read of the Dalton marriage—I do not find it difficult to believe that Adeline considered divorcing Lewis, even though she did not follow through on the idea.

Chapter 3: The Lawmen

Nancy B. Samuelson's 1992 book, *The Dalton Gang Story*, serves as the principal source for this chapter. Most of the following information about the Daltons as outlaws comes from this work. Other sources used are indicated in the text.

The four Daltons who served the law were Frank, Grat, Bob, and Emmett. Frank, the older brother who was much admired by the younger Daltons, was appointed a U. S. deputy marshal in 1884.[1] He worked out of Fort Smith, Arkansas, for Judge Isaac Parker, the "hanging judge." Being a marshal was dangerous and not very lucrative, even by 1880 standards. Frank received $2.00 for every outlaw he caught, and he sometimes didn't get the money for a long time (Dary 123). Killed in November 1887 when he attempted to arrest three bootleggers in Indian Territory, Frank is buried in Elmwood Cemetery in Coffeyville (Samuelson 53)[2]

Perhaps hoping to avenge their brother's death, the three younger Daltons became lawmen. Sworn in as a deputy marshal, Grat was quickly reminded that a deputy's job was dangerous. In March 1889, as part of a posse trying to make an arrest, he was wounded and another lawman killed (78). Bob became a posseman working under Grat, and then was himself appointed a deputy marshal. Emmett went to work for Bob as a guard. Bob also at some point served as a detective for the Osage Indian Agency headquartered at Pawhuska (79).

No records have been found that definitely establish when the Daltons resigned as lawmen. McKennon wrote that the brothers resigned in 1890 over an argument about wages (12). A March 13, 1890, *Indian Chieftain* article lent credence to the idea that Grat at least was still a deputy in early 1890 (Samuelson 80-81).

Numerous accounts of the Dalton brothers said Grat, Bob, and Emmett were already leaning toward their outlaw ways while working for the law. Samuelson has done an impressive job of researching court records, contemporary newspapers, and various other old documents. Her conclusion is that some of the stories of their illegal behavior while serving as lawmen are completely false, while others are questionable (79). Some of the stories follow.

Two of the oft-told stories involved shootings. In December of 1888 Bob Dalton shot and killed Charley Montgomery. Some accounts said Montgomery had run off with Bob's girlfriend (Dary 123). Others said that Bob killed Montgomery in the line of duty.[3] Samuelson includes an article from the August 16, 1888, *Coffeyville Journal* which probably comes as close to the truth as is possible after so many years. Charley Montgomery was a wanted man, though he seems not to have been considered particularly dangerous. Posseman Bob Dalton, with guards Al Landis and Bill Griggs, went to arrest Montgomery. Montgomery resisted arrest, opening fire. His first shot took off a small portion of one of Landis's ears. Next he fired at Bob Dalton at such close range that some powder lodged in the posseman's face. Dalton then fired his shotgun, and Montgomery fell dead (65-66).

The second shooting occurred a few months later. Bob shot the young son of Alex Cochran in Claremore, Indian Territory. Some versions of this story said the three Daltons were after the elder Cochran, an Indian who had wounded a lawman who had been trying to arrest him. They shot and severely wounded Cochran's young son by mistake (Preece 55-56).

Samuelson again offers a contemporary account, this time from *The Indian Chieftain* of Vinita, Oklahoma. The April 17, 1890, issue revealed that Bob Cox, a posseman, was wounded while trying to arrest Bud Maxfield and a cohort named Halm, who were recent escapees from the penitentiary. Learning the escapees were at a dance, Cox and a helper went to the dance and purchased some whiskey from Ed Louthers. (Louthers was acting as a delivery boy for Halm, who was selling illegal whiskey out of a barn loft.) Cox had handcuffed Louthers and was preparing to seek out Halm when young Jess Cochran and his father Alex decided to help Louthers. One of them shot Cox in the neck and shoulder. Several other shots were fired back and forth. Cox was again wounded, this time in the thigh. Cox had to withdraw because of his wounds. The handcuffed Louthers ran away during the gunfight. The next morning Jess Cochran, on his way home from town, was spotted by posseman Bob Dalton. Dalton called upon young Cochran to halt. When Cochran continued on his way, the posseman fired, "killing the horse and shooting the boy through the leg" (67-68).

Yet other stories about the Daltons as lawmen involved whiskey. Dary said that the Daltons would slip whiskey into the wagons of settlers traveling into Indian Territory, where whiskey was not allowed. When the lawmen would stop the settlers, they would impose a fine for the concealed whiskey, a fine that never was reported to Fort Smith (123). Samuelson says Heck Thomas, a frontier marshal, claimed such stories were constantly told about deputy marshals, but he never knew of a case where the stories were true. "According to Heck there was simply no need for an officer to go to such expense and trouble when plenty of whiskey could be located without such effort" (81).

Much speculation has occurred about the Dalton's first crime. What was their first illegal act, the act that eventually led to the shootout at Coffeyville?[4]

The first document which offered any support for the charge that the Daltons broke the law while still employed as lawmen was a warrant for the arrest of Bob and Emmett and two others on the charge of introducing whiskey into Indian Territory on December 25, 1889. On that date all three Daltons may still have been lawmen. Deputy L. Shadley arrested Bob and Emmett on March 21, 1890. At their March 26 hearing, seven Osages testified as witnesses. In none of the undated statements from witnesses did anyone testify that Bob sold liquor to the Indians. The charges against Emmett were dropped, but Bob was bound over to appear at district court in September. Released on bail, Bob didn't show up for his September trial (Samuelson 81-82).

Samuelson sums up the issue as follows:

> It is difficult to draw any definite conclusions about Bob Dalton's guilt from the documents that still exist. ... It is entirely possible that Bob had indulged in the "fire water" himself to the point he was in no condition to arrest anyone else for selling booze that day. ... it was Christmas .... What is obvious is that Bob Dalton would still have been wanted on the Introducing charge and for failing to appear for trial when trouble again arose for the Daltons in September 1890. (82)

Numerous versions of the Dalton brothers' activities stated the brothers had difficulty receiving their wages from the government. This seems to have been the truth. Samuelson includes information from government documents showing that for five months Bob Dalton did not receive any of the wages due him. This problem was not unique to the Daltons. Other records show that in 1895 one former deputy was still trying to collect $550 owed him for four years of service (85-86).

Whatever their reasons for giving up on the law, the Daltons, by September 1890, had stepped across the line that separates lawmen from outlaws.

Notes to Chapter 3: The Lawmen

1   Burton Rascoe, in the Introduction to *The Dalton Brothers by an Eye Witness*, wrote that he could find no proof that Frank Dalton was killed in the performance of his duty or even that Frank was ever a U. S. deputy marshal (21). He must not have looked very hard for such proof. I only include Rascoe's comments to illustrate how many false ideas have been circulated about the Daltons.

2   Samuelson points out that Frank's tombstone incorrectly lists 1888 as the year of his death (48).

3   This shooting, with its background of ill-fated romance, has generated a great many wild stories over the years. The romance itself is part of the fiction. No reputable documentation of the existence of Minnie Johnson—or of any other girl friend of Bob's—has been found.

   The Dalton Brothers by an Eye Witness said that Bob Dalton and Minnie Johnson were sweethearts until Charley Montgomery stole Minnie's heart. Minnie and Montgomery ran off together. When Montgomery returned some weeks later to pick up his things, he was shot in the back (59-68). *Eye Witness* wrote "the treachery of his first love threw Bob Dalton into that criminal existence which was to end in his tragic death" (68).

   McLoughlin had a slightly different version of this story. He wrote that Bob waylaid Montgomery the next spring and killed him with a shot in the back of his head. Bob's explanation for the shooting was that he had caught Montgomery stealing horses (127).

Preece repeated the same story, except he has Bob, with the help of Emmett, taking the body to Lang and Lape, Coffeyville undertakers. In this version, the Daltons told Mr. Lang that Montgomery had been caught stealing some horse gear from a stable on a ranch in Indian Territory. Bob claimed he had shot Montgomery when he tried to evade arrest (44).

Emmett, in *Beyond the Law*, said Montgomery was killed near Coffeyville in Timberhills when U. S. Marshal Yoe sent Bob to pick up Montgomery. There was a warrant for Montgomery's arrest for robbing Jacob Bartles's store. Al Landers, a posseman, went with Bob. They found Montgomery near Lon Brown's cabin. Montgomery shot at the lawmen, then turned and ran around the cabin. Bob had also started around the cabin when the two men ran into each other. Two shots were fired, and Montgomery fell dead (21-22). This version seems much closer to what probably happened than was customary for Emmett.

4   We've already seen that T*he Dalton Brothers by an Eyewitness* said his first love's treachery and his subsequent killing of Montgomery were Bob's first crime. (See note 2.) However, eleven pages later *Eyewitness* indicated that Bob's "first downward step" was selling whiskey to the Indians (79).

The 1903 *History of Montgomery County, Kansas* said the Daltons first venture into crime was stealing a herd of cattle in 1890 (34).

McNeal wrote that Bob's first illegal act was "selling protection to outlaws" (271).

Emmett, in *When the Daltons Rode*, detailed yet another first crime. He said Bob, George Newcomb, Charley Bryant, William McElhanie, and he got involved in a faro game somewhere between Silver City and Santa Rosa, New Mexico. When they discovered the game was crooked, they took back their money at gunpoint and helped themselves to the other money in the game (2-7). Emmett wrote "The charter members of the Dalton band had set out upon their extensive career of outlawry" (5).

Nash repeated Emmett's claim that sticking up the faro game in New Mexico was the brothers' first step outside the law (145).

Preece (58) and Dary (123) said that the horsetheft incident was the venture that turned the Daltons into outlaws (See the next chapter). Littleton agreed (Latta 48).

Ben Dalton, in an October 27, 1892, article in the *San Francisco Chronicle,* said that the perjured testimony presented against his brothers in the Alila train robbery trial (See the next chapter) was the last straw that definitely turned his brothers to crime. Their first actual crime, according to Ben, involved accepting money from some whiskey smugglers who offered it as a bribe to ward off arrest (Samuelson 97-99).

Chapter 4: The Outlaws

Samuelson's 1992 book, *The Dalton Gang Story*, also serves as the principal source for this chapter. Most of the following information about the Daltons as outlaws comes from this work. Other sources used are indicated in the text.

Being a lawman and being an outlaw are at opposite ends of the same spectrum: different yet similar. Since Grat was appointed deputy marshal after Frank's death in 1887, and probably served at least until March 1890, it seems likely that he was a lawman at least as long as he was an outlaw. The same might be claimed for Bob and Emmett. However, it is for their brief months as outlaws that Grat, Bob, and Emmett Dalton are remembered.

Stealing horses was one of the crimes attributed to the Daltons. They supposedly would steal horses in Indian Territory and sell them across the line in Kansas. The May 8, 1891, *Fort Smith Elevator* contained what may be the original version of the horse stealing stories. Samuelson reprints the actual newspaper article. It stated that at some time after July 4, 1890, Bob and Emmett stole several horses and mules in the Osage Nation and sold them in the Cherokee Nation to Emmett Vann, a rancher.[1] Their second venture was said to be stealing a group of horses from Bob Rogers and Frank Musgrove near Claremore, Indian Territory. Those horses Bob and Emmett sold at Columbus, Kansas, to a dealer named Scott. Next they supposedly gathered another group of someone else's horses in the Osage Nation and ran them up into Kansas, again intending to sell to Scott, this time at Baxter Springs. The Daltons were said to have arrived at Baxter just as Rogers and Musgrove had convinced Scott that the first group of horses had been stolen from them. Bob and Emmett narrowly escaped the furious stockmen (82-84).[2]

The *Elevator* account claimed that only Bob and Emmett were involved in these horsethefts. However, by September 8, 1890, Grat was under arrest for stealing fourteen horses from Rogers and Musgrove. Samuelson has looked up the actual court records, which showed a hearing was held on September 18 and 19 at Fort Smith. Grat was bound over and ordered to deposit bail of $1,000 or await his trial in jail. On September 25, Grat was still in jail, so he obviously couldn't make bail. Samuelson writes "It appears that later the charges were dropped and he was released. There is no record at all of charges against Bob or Emmett for this supposed horse stealing incident" (85). At this point, one hundred and two years later, we probably will never know whether or not the Daltons were guilty of stealing horses, but we can be fairly certain they were not convicted.

Whether or not the Daltons actually sold whiskey in Indian Territory or stole horses, we can be confident they did rob some trains. Emmett, who was chary of making himself seem like a true outlaw, in *When the Daltons Rode*, discussed four train robberies that he participated in. Chances are the Daltons were innocent, however, of the first train robbery with which they are usually credited.

The mighty Southern Pacific railroad, in the process of monopolizing California's transportation industry, had made many enemies in California and elsewhere. Violence had occurred when the Southern Pacific reneged on agreements made to settlers on its land grants. Samuelson details a portion of this retaliation:

Then came what some historians have called the SP [Southern Pacific] War. Between February 1889 and August 1892 five SP trains were robbed. All five robberies were committed by two men, usually masked, and the method of operation was basically the same for all. (87)

Those Southern Pacific robberies occurred on February 22, 1889; January 20, 1890; February 6, 1891; September 3, 1891; and August 3, 1892 (87).

We know the Daltons were in Indian Territory during the first two robberies. Grat was still in jail in September of 1890. Sometime between September 1890 and February 1891, the brothers traveled west to visit their brothers Bill, Littleton, Ben, and Cole, who had settled in California. This visit was bad timing on the part of Grat, Bob, and Emmett.

Here's a brief summary of events during and after the third Southern Pacific train robbery. On February 6, 1891, at Alila, California, outlaws attempted a train holdup. During the robbery, both the train's fireman and the Wells Fargo agent were wounded in a gunbattle. The fireman died the next day (88).

The Southern Pacific detectives, unable to find the outlaws who had robbed the first two trains, learned that the three Oklahoma Dalton brothers were in California visiting. Knowing of the Dalton/Younger relationship, railroad authorities decided to make an example of the Daltons. Grat Dalton and his brother Bill were eventually arrested and charged with the Alila robbery. Both Daltons protested their innocence.[3] Samuelson's book again demonstrates her diligent research. Interested readers should by all means consult her Chapter V for additional information about the California episode.

An interesting fact not brought out in the Dalton trials was that on February 11th Wells Fargo agent Haswell was indicted for manslaughter for accidentally shooting fireman Radliff during the Alila gun battle with the robbers. Haswell was arraigned on March 19th. After that the case against Haswell just disappeared from court documents (88).[4]

Court records showed that four Daltons—Grat, Bob, Emmett, and Bill—were indicted on March 17, 1891, for "Assult with intent to commit murder upon one C. C. Haswell [the Wells Fargo agent] and assult with intent to commit robbery [sic]" (89) Though the Daltons could hardly be charged with the murder of fireman Radliff—since Haswell had been arraigned for that shooting—Samuelson says several speeches during the course of Grat's trial implied that the fireman had been shot by the Daltons (94).

Testimony at Grat's trial, which began June 17, 1891, was "confusing and contradictory" (92). Some witnesses admitted that the railroad was paying their expenses during the trial and that Southern Pacific detectives had helped them remember events surrounding the robbery. All the evidence presented at the trial "had been in the hands of the railroad or Wells Fargo personnel for some time, most of it for several months.." (93).

The powerful hand of the Southern Pacific seemed to hover over the witnesses, the evidence, and the judge. W. A. Gray, who had represented Haswell at his indictment, was suddenly appointed a second superior judge for Tulare County (the appointment arrived by telegram) and presided over Grat's trial. Although both the prosecuting attorney and the defense attorney requested that a complete transcript be kept of the trial, the presiding judge refused. When the trial ended on July 9, 1891, Grat was found guilty (94). He was scheduled to be sentenced the end of July. Grat avoided what would have been a twenty-year prison sentence by escaping from jail and hightailing it back to Oklahoma.[5]

After Grat's conviction, Bill's bail was reduced from $30,000 to $5,000. He was able to arrange for this amount, so he was released on bail. When another train was held up on September 3, the Southern Pacific took after Bill for the new robbery, though he was still out on bail awaiting trial for the Alila robbery. Bill came to his own defense on September 17 in the *Tulare County Times*.

> Now just consider how improbable a story that is. Here everyone says I am a desperate and shrewd man. I have the ability to plan a train robbery and the courage to execute it. Yet I would be such a fool as to go in broad daylight, and be seen within a few miles of the scene of the robbery. ... The whole story is so absurd that no one but a Southern Pacific detective could ever conceive it. (Samuelson 95)

Bill was returned to jail, but this time the newspapers had caught on that the Southern Pacific wasn't playing fair. During Bill's trial, which was held in October, one Southern Pacific detective admitted that he had lied to Bill several times. Another admitted that he had asked the Daltons' bondsmen to cancel their bond so that Bill would have to return to jail. Thirteen area residents testified as character witnesses for Bill. When his trial ended, the verdict was "Not Guilty" (95-96).

While Grat and Bill were trying to cope with the Southern Pacific in California, Bob and Emmett got busy back in Indian Territory, busy robbing trains. Horan said the Daltons wanted to get even with the express companies that had falsely charged them with the Alila robbery (150). Emmett wrote that Bob and he worked with George Newcomb and Charley Bryant on the plans for a train robbery near Wharton (*Beyond the Law* 57).[6] They toyed with the idea of going to South America if they made a big enough haul.

On May 11, 1891, near Wharton, Indian Territory, the four held up a Santa Fe train.[7] Samuelson prints several newspaper accounts of the robbery and the subsequent manhunt. The May 14, 1891, *Muskogee Phoenix* reported that the robbery netted the outlaws $500. Only the express car was robbed. The outlaws told the passengers to stay in their coaches so they wouldn't be hurt (101-02). The *Fort Smith Elevator* of May 15, 1891, reported that the railroad claimed to have lost $1,500 in the robbery (102).[8]

Dalton accomplice Charley Bryant was captured by deputy Ed Short in the middle of August. While being transported to Wichita by train, he attempted to escape. An August 27 *Indian Chieftain* article stated, "the prisoner, who was in the baggage car, got possession of a pistol and a fight ensued in which both [Bryant and deputy Short] were killed" (Samuelson 104).

Although surely upset by Bryant's death, the Daltons struck again in September, this time holding up a Missouri, Kansas and Texas (Katy) train at Lillietta, near Waggoner. Emmett wrote that he and Bob were again joined by Newcomb, whose nickname was "Bitter Creek." Charley Pierce, Bill Doolin, Dick Broadwell, and Bill Power made up the rest of the gang (*When the Daltons Rode* 129).[9] The *Fort Smith Elevator* of September 18th announced the Lillietta train had been robbed of $2,500 to $3,000 (Samuelson 106).[10]

Rumors about the Daltons flew everywhere. People reported seeing the gang's camp on one side of the Grand River; another camp was spotted on the other side of the river; a third camp supposedly was seen east of Pryor. Almost every unlawful act of the time was laid at the feet of the Dalton gang. Charles Carpenter, one of those Coffeyville citizens who was to survive the Coffeyville raid, writing about 1938, said, "Every reported holdup from Missouri to Wyoming was charged to the gang" (24). Carpenter went on to say that the Katy Railroad had offered a reward of $5,000 for each member of the Dalton gang (24).

Grat was back from California in time for the gang's third train robbery in June 1892. This time they held up a Santa Fe train at Red Rock. The June 10, 1892, *Fort Smith Elevator* reported the gang may have made away with about $70,000 (Samuelson 109).[11]

The July 14, 1892, train robbery was to be their last. The gang held up a Katy train at Adair, Indian Territory. The outlaws held the depot agent at gun point and waited for the train, which had secretly been boarded by armed guards.[12] A gunfight ensued. The July 21 *Indian Chieftain* reported that five men were wounded, one of them dying later. (The dead man's wound may well have come from a random shot from one of the guards.) The outlaws apparently escaped without injury (Samuelson 109-11). The *Kingfisher Free Press* of July 21, 1892, reported the amount taken to be in the neighborhood of $40,000 (Samuelson 112-13).

Thus we have the outlaw career of Grat, Bob, and Emmett Dalton. In March of 1890 Bob was charged with introducing liquor into Indian Territory, but jumped bail and didn't appear for his trial. In September of 1890 Grat was arrested for stealing horses, but either the charges were dropped or he was released. Grat was convicted of a California train robbery that it's highly likely he had no part in. He escaped before being sent to the penitentiary. Then the Daltons, with several cohorts, robbed four trains between May of 1891 and mid-July of 1892. Only during the last train robbery was anyone shot, and the deadly wound on that occasion may well have come from a stray bullet.

At this point the nearest the brothers had come to robbing a bank was robbing a Wells Fargo express car with one, perhaps two, agents inside. Now, in October of 1892, less than three months after their last train robbery, the Daltons headed toward Coffeyville, toward its two banks, and toward its death alley.

Notes to Chapter 4: The Outlaws

1   At this period Indian Territory was divided into approximately twenty different Indian nations and some unassigned lands. The April 22, 1889, Oklahoma land run had allowed white settlers to settle and homestead some of those unassigned lands.

2   Littleton (Latta 48-49) and Preece (58-59) both repeated the information from the May 8, 1891, *Fort Smith Elevator*.

   Dary's version was only slightly different. It said that when the Daltons took the horses belonging to the Cherokee Indian (Rogers was a Cherokee) from Claremore, I. T., the Indian, got up a posse and followed the gang. The posse caught up with the Daltons near Baxter Springs. The Daltons fled, and the Indian got his horses back (123).

3   Latta's work showed that Littleton believed his brothers had committed the Alila robbery (54-66). However, Littleton didn't talk with Latta about his brothers until after Emmett died in 1937. Littleton was born in 1857, so he was eighty by the time Latta was gathering information from him. In addition, Samuelson cites a letter from sister Leona Dalton to Latta: "We believe any information that Littleton gives out could hardly be considered authentic as he has not been in touch with the family for over 42 years and for only a short time at that having gone west at 16 years of age and only back home twice" (44).

4   It's probably noteworthy here that the Southern Pacific owned Wells Fargo (88).

5   *The Dalton Brothers by An Eyewitness* had a wild tale about Grat's escape. He supposedly was being transported to the penitentiary on the train. He was handcuffed and accompanied

by two guards. When one of his guards was at the end of the car and the other was drowsing, Grat jumped up; his handcuffs fell from his wrists, and he leaped through the open train window—while the train was going forty-five miles an hour—into a stream. When the deputies searched the area, they found hoofprints, indicating the escape had been prearranged (99). (Author's note: If this story is true, Grat was a magician as well as an Olympic acrobat.)

Preece wrote that Grat escaped, with two other prisoners from the jail, three days before he was to be sentenced (102).

Latta, using information from one of the Tulare County's ex-deputies, wrote that Grat used a file and a hacksaw to effect his escape. The deputies found pieces of them after Grat was gone (134).

In *When the Daltons Rode*, Emmett said that Grat got a hacksaw blade from a Negro trusty. After cutting through the bars, Grat and three others picked up a rifle from a spot near the jail where an accomplice had hidden it for him (112-14).

The real escape might have been easier than all of the above. Samuelson points out it was revealed during the trial that Grat had a key that might have worked in at least some of the jail doors (94).

6   Emmett also wrote that Bob's girlfriend, Eugenia Moore, helped with the robbery by furnishing information about what train would be carrying large sums (*Beyond the Law* 57). Eugenia, like *Eyewitness*'s tale about Minnie Johnson mentioned in the preceding chapter, was a complete invention on the part of Emmett.

7   Breihan inserted a new accomplice and a new date. He said that Bob and Emmett Dalton, Bill Doolin, and Charlie Bryant robbed the Wharton train on May 8th (20).

McKennon wrote that Bill Doolin, Bill Power, and Dick Broadwell were also with the Daltons during the Wharton robbery (12).

A June 1891 *Coffeyville Journal* article said the Daltons, an outlaw called Six Shooter Jack, and a young man named Norton were suspected in the Wharton robbery (Huff "100 Years Ago" 5).

8   In *When the Daltons Rode*, Emmett claimed they netted about $14,000 in the Wharton robbery (97).

9   Although Emmett and others spelled the name Powers, Samuelson shows that the correct spelling is Power, without the *s* (100).

10 In *When the Daltons Rode*, Emmett wrote their haul from the Lillietta robbery was a bit over $19,000 (135). He had evidently forgotten that in *Beyond the Law*, written earlier, he had claimed they netted something over $7,000 (97).

11 Horan reported the Red Rock robbery netted the gang about $11,000 (151).

12 Branson and Branson wrote that a farmer noticed the Dalton gang riding toward Adair and notified the deputy marshal. The marshal got a nine-man posse together. This posse boarded the train before it got to Adair and stayed hidden in the smoking car (62).

Chapter 5: The Approach

D. Stewart Elliott's book, *Last Raid of the Daltons*, published in 1892, and his newspaper account of the raid published on October 7, 1892, are the principal sources for this chapter. Elliott, editor of the *Journal*, was an eyewitness to the raid and was known to the Daltons. Because of the brevity of his works, individual page numbers are cited only for direct quotes. Any other sources used are indicated in the text.

Those locations printed in boldface type at their first mention can be found in *Figure 5.1. Map of the Plaza Area in 1892.*

On the afternoon of October 4, 1892, a group of men cut a barbed wire fence and rode across a plowed field, five abreast, to some timber near Onion Creek on the P.L. Davis farm. Davis's residence was three miles southwest of Coffeyville. They tied their horses to separate trees and prepared to camp.[1] Then two rode to a nearby cornfield belonging to Mrs. J. F. Savage, where they gathered corn for their horses. They fed the horses, and the men ate a lunch of biscuits and hardboiled eggs, remnants of which were found several days later. The men who made up this group from that day on would always be called the Dalton gang. The actual Daltons were Grat, Bob, and Emmett. Their cohorts were Bill Power (sometimes known as Tom Evans) and Richard L. (Dick) Broadwell (sometimes known as John Moore or Texas Jack).

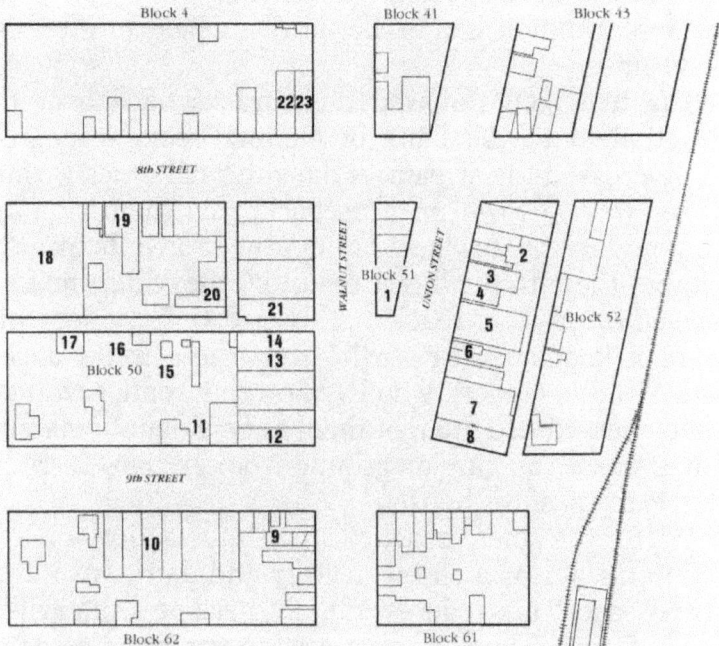

1. C.M. Condon & Company Bank
2. Cubine's Boot and Shoe Shop
3. Rammel Brothers Drug
4. First National Bank
5. Isham Brothers & Mansur Hardware
6. Smith's Barber Shop
7. Barndollar Brothers Store
8. A.P. Boswell & Company Hardware
9. Suthard and Blease Boot and Shoe Shop
10. Swisher Brothers Machine Shop
11. Lewark & Kloehr Livery Service
12. Read Brothers Store
13. Lang and Lape Undertakers and Furniture
14. Slosson & Company Drug
    (Dr. Wells's Office was over Slosson Drug.)
15. City Jail
16. Stable
17. Police Judge Charles Munn's lot
18. Long Bell Lumber Company
19. Davis Blacksmith Shop
20. Farmer's Home Boarding House
21. McKenna and Adamson's Store
22. Ullom's Restaurant
23. McCoy's Hardware

Figure 5.1.
Map of Plaza Area in 1892

Figure 5.1. Map of Plaza Area in 1892

October 5 dawned a bright, clear Wednesday. When the men left the timber, two of them looked different. Bob, the leader, was wearing a heavy black moustache and goatee. Grat sported a black moustache and side whiskers. Emmett had earlier grown a beard to wear as his disguise.[2]

The five men followed their tracks back over the plowed field to the bank of Onion Creek, where the bridge crossed the stream. A daughter of James Brown, on her way to town on horseback, saw them ride out from under the bridge and up the north bank. She followed them to the direct road to Coffeyville; she then traveled on up that road, east toward Coffeyville, while the men kept straight north, over a less well-traveled road. William Gilbert, who lived on that road, saw them as they passed. He thought them to be a deputy marshal with a posse, as similar groups from Indian Territory often came past his house.

When the men reached the intersection of two section lines near a cheese factory and dairy farm, they turned east. This road eventually became Coffeyville's Eighth Street. The road was dry, so the five horsemen raised dust as they trotted down the road. Mr. and Mrs. R.H. Hollingsworth, who were driving west, passed the men less than a mile west of the city limits. John M. and J.L. Seldomridge, also driving west, passed the group just before it reached the city limits. Both the Hollingsworths and the Seldomridges stated there were six men in the party, all heavily armed. Other individuals who saw the men as they moved closer to the center of town stated that there were only five in the group.[3]

The group continued east on Eighth, with the three Daltons in front and Power and Broadwell in the rear, until they reached the corner of Eighth and Maple, where the Episcopal church was located. Here they turned south. They passed the **Long-Bell Lumber Company**'s office and turned east into the alley that runs through block 50 from Maple to Walnut.[4]

An account in the *Journal* published two days after the raid implied the gang had planned to leave their horses at the hitching racks north of **Ulloms Restaurant** and in front of **McCoys**.[5] However, they found the street there all torn up and the hitching posts gone. Whatever the actual case, the Dalton gang did ride into the alley, stopping at the rear of **Police Judge Charles Munn's lot**. Here they dismounted, tying their horses to the fence at the north end of Munn's property, about 50 feet east of Maple, and about 350 feet from Walnut street. The alley was bustling; several teams of horses were tied in the back of the **Davis Blacksmith Shop**.

Figure 5.2. Death Alley Fence where Outlaws tied their Horses

The five walked east toward the plaza, three in front and two in back. A stonecutter, checking out some rock that was piled near the **City Jail** which opened onto the alley, noticed that they were carrying guns under their garments. Thinking nothing of it, he dropped in behind them.

Figure 5.3. City Jail on South Side of Alley

The gang and the stonecutter passed along the north side of **Slosson & Co. Drug Store** and the south side of the **McKenna and Adamson's** dry-goods store as they neared the alley entrance on Walnut Street. The gang started east across Walnut, and the stonecutter went north to his work further up the block.

Figure 5.4. The East Side of Walnut

A Consolidated Company oil tank wagon drawn by two horses turned into the alley from Walnut at about the time the group left the alley, approximately 9:30 A.M. This wagon parked in the alley about 100 feet west of Walnut. J. P. Moran was driving the tankwagon; he was there to make a delivery to Slosson's ("Daltons!" 2D).

Notes to Chapter 5: The Approach

1 Carpenter's account said the gang camped on Allin's Hill the night before the robbery. Allin's Hill is three miles west of Coffeyville on Onion Creek, so his account had the camp located a bit further north than does Elliott's (24).

Figure 5.5. Rock found near Allin's Hill

This rock was found in the 1980s buried along Onion Creek near Allin's Hill. No claim can be made about its authenticity, but the carving does resemble the carving in pictures of a Dalton hideout in Indian Territory. Bob's saddle was decorated with hearts. A heart or shield is carved to the right of the date on the rock.

2 Carpenter wrote that only Grat was disguised (24).

3 The sixth rider has been an issue for many writers. Below are only a few of the many theories.

Graves said that Bill Doolin had planned to go with the Daltons, but a lame horse delayed him (54).

Adams, in *Six Guns*, said that Bill Doolin was still a member of the Dalton gang in 1892 but felt the Coffeyville plan was rash. He chose not to take part (280). Adams went on to say that it was only after the death of the Daltons in the Coffeyville raid that Doolin organized his own gang (472). In *Burs*, however, Adams wrote that Doolin would have been with the gang except his horse had gone lame (116).

Aley (some writers spelled this Ally) Ogee was charged with being the sixth rider but was able to provide an alibi for October 5 (Pannill 13).

Latta believed Emmett didn't reveal who the sixth rider was because of loyalty to a fellow outlaw. Latta wrote "It generally has been agreed that because of a lame horse Bill Dalton was forced to leave the gang and retreat into Oklahoma" (222).

Elliott mentioned the sixth outlaw in the newspaper account (6) but omitted any reference to him in *Last Raid*. This may indicate that he had decided the accounts of the sixth rider were merely occasioned by the general excitement.

W. H. Tibbils of Vinita, Indian Territory, wrote a letter to Elliott stating that he had consulted with the Indian Police, the Vinita city marshal, and Deputy U.S. Marshal L. P. Isabell. All were positive there had been only five members of the Dalton gang throughout 1892. Tibbils was convinced the scare about a sixth gang member was created by railroad detectives Thomas and Dodge. He believed the two detectives wanted the citizenry to worry about additional gang members' being around so that they could justify their salaries. He described Thomas and Dodge as men "who could always be found where the Daltons were not."

Thomas C. Babb, one of the Condon employees, many years later told a reporter he had seen a sixth man escape ("Daltons! 81). Babb's memory had probably been clouded by time. If a sixth outlaw had actually been on the plaza, others would have seen him.

The wildest explanation of the sixth "man" came from Pannill's booklet. In it he argued that the sixth rider was Florence Quick. He then went on to claim that Florence Quick was really Eugenia Moore. Finally he tried to convince the reader that

Florence Quick was a name Emmett used to disguise the fact that his wife, Julia Johnson, was with the Daltons as they approached Coffeyville. (I'm certainly not convinced by Pannill's explanation, and I find it hard to believe that anyone else who had read much about the Daltons would be either.)

4   Latta said the group traveled south on Union Street coming into town and then turned west on Eighth to Maple (208-10). He might have been misled by Emmett's account (*When the Daltons Rode* 237). Too many people saw the gang on Eighth to make the Union entry an option. Also, had they come in on Union, why did they go to Maple before turning south and entering the alley from the west? It would have been more logical to turn south on Walnut and enter the alley from the east.

5   Emmett said the group had planned to tie their horses to the hitching rails in front of the opera house. He said the front of the opera house was on Eighth, and the back jutted up against the back of the Condon bank. However, when they arrived, they found these hitching rails were down (*When the Daltons Rode* 237-38).

The 1890 map of downtown Coffeyville does not show the opera house where Emmett said it was; perhaps he'd remembered a different location from his earlier days in Coffeyville. Before the 1885 fire, the Wells Brothers building had been described as a merchant establishment and an opera house, and there were other locations used as opera houses at various times (*Coffeyville at 100* 20).

Chapter 6: The Raid

Elliott's book, *Last Raid of the Daltons*, published in 1892, and his newspaper account of the raid published on October 7, 1892, are the principal sources for this chapter. Again, because of the brevity of his works, individual page numbers are cited only for direct quotes. Any other sources used are indicated in the text.

As occurs elsewhere, the locations printed in boldface type at their first mention can be found *in Figure 5.1. Map of the Plaza Area in 1892.*

Before 8:00 AM that Wednesday the streets around the plaza were filled with people bringing produce to the community and with those on errands typical of a busy town in a rural area. Some people walked, some were on horseback, and some were in wagons or buggies.

Aleck McKenna was standing in front of McKenna and Adamson's dry-goods store when the Dalton gang came out of the alley. They passed within five feet of him, and he noticed their disguises. Recognizing one of the Daltons by his walk and the shape of his head, McKenna watched as the first three men went into the **C. M. Condon & Co. Bank**'s southwest door and as the other two ran across the street and entered the **First National Bank**. The plate glass front of the Condon Bank faced south; it had two entrances, one on either side. Double doors opened onto Walnut from the southwest front and onto Union from the southeast front. Both of these entrances had glass in their upper halves.

Figure 6.1. The Condon Bank in 1892

From where he was standing, McKenna had a clear view into the front part of the Condon. To his amazement he saw a Winchester pointed toward the cashier's counter. He quickly called out to the men in the dry goods' store that the bank was being robbed. After the initial alarm, it's certain that people at different points of the plaza excitedly passed the news around.[1] Though some accounts of the day implied that Coffeyville had been forewarned of the raid, *Journal* Editor Elliott quite positively stated that was untrue; at the time the alarm was given, there "was not an armed man any where " [sic] around (*Last Raid* 26).[2]

Citizens seeking to halt the robbery ran to the two hardware stores on the plaza to arm themselves. The **A.P. Boswell & Co** hardware was in a two-story brick building on Union at the southeast corner of the plaza area. The **Isham Brothers & Mansur** hardware store was a large one-story brick building on the east side of Union immediately south of the First National Bank.[3] Both stores, which had firearm inventories, passed out guns and ammunition to people who sought to stop the robbery. George Cubine, in **Cubine's Boot and Shoe Shop**, three doors north of the First National Bank, snatched his Winchester from its place on the wall and rushed to help ("In Memoriam"). With the exception of Cubine's Winchester, all of the guns used by the citizens were supplied by either Isham's or Boswell's.

The **Lewark & Kloehr Livery Service**, on Ninth Street, stretched from the north side of Ninth back to the alley dividing block 50. John J. Kloehr, liveryman, was one of the citizens who picked up a rifle at Boswell and Co. Someone handed him a Winchester, and Kloehr went behind the counter to pick out the needed ammunition and load the gun. He and some others then went out onto the sidewalk in front of Boswell's. A dozen citizens with rifles and shotguns quickly erected a barricade from wagons standing in front of Boswell's. From this vantage point they had a clear view into the front of the Condon.

The **Barndollar Brothers** store was between Isham's and Boswell's on Union. Parker L. Williams got a Colt .44 revolver from Boswell's and climbed out on

Barndollar's awning so he would have a good field of fire.

Figure 6.2. Cubine's Boot and Shoe Shop

Isham's two front entrances on Union were sheltered by an awning supported by iron columns. Both entrances stood open that October morning. Inside, Henry H. Isham and two clerks, Lewis A. Dietz and T. Arthur Reynolds, were waiting on customers. Charles T Gump, a drayman driving his team on Union when the alarm was raised, hurried into Isham's and chose a double-barreled shotgun from the store's inventory. Hurrying back out onto the sidewalk, Gump positioned himself behind an awning post. He faced north, toward the First National Bank, and waited for the outlaws to leave the bank. From this vantage point he could also see the front area of the Condon and the alley on the west side of the plaza. Storeowner Isham closed the store's safe, grabbed a rifle, and went to stand near a large steel stove in the front of the store. Dietz picked up a revolver and stood near Isham.

Lucius M Baldwin, a 23 year-old clerk in **Read Brothers**, started toward the door when he heard the alarm. Haz Read warned the young man not to go out (Green). Not heeding the warning, Baldwin walked across to Isham's and picked up a snub-nosed revolver.

While Coffeyville's citizens were arming themselves, the three of the Dalton gang in the Condon Bank were unaware that the alarm had been given. Charles T. Carpenter, a bank officer, had been at the west side of the front counter when the gang entered. Thomas C. Babb, the bookkeeper, had been sitting at a desk on the east side near the vault. Charles M. Ball, Cashier, had been in an office on the northwest side of the bank. This office, which opened into the front of the bank, also had a door which led into a back entry with an exit onto Walnut Street and a stairway leading up to offices. A customer, John D. Levan, came into the bank through the southwest door at about this time. The gunmen in the front of the bank told him to lie down on the floor.[4]

Carpenter hadn't seen the Daltons as they had come in the southwest door, but had turned to see Grat's Winchester pointed at him. Grat swore, yelling at the bank employees to hold up their hands. Bill Power went over to the southwest door, and Dick Broadwell went to stand by the southeast door. The gang had not yet seen Babb, the bookkeeper, who quietly moved into the vault.

The Cashier, hearing the commotion, came into the front of the bank and discovered the Winchesters covering him and Carpenter. Grat went through the private office and entered the area behind the bank counter. He gave Cashier Ball a two-bushel grain sack, telling him to hold it open, and directed Carpenter to put all the money on the counter and in the cash drawer into the sack, which he did.[5]

Carpenter here included an incident not found in other accounts. He wrote that Luther Perkins, whose office was over the Condon, had seen Bob and Emmett go into the First National. He hurried down the stairs which led both to the back entrance on Walnut and to the back door of the Condon, opened the door, and called out to Carpenter. Seeing the bank employees covered by rifles, Perkins slammed the door shut and hurried back to his office upstairs where Joe Uncapher and J. H. Wilcox were excitedly staring out at the plaza area and the activity around Isham's and Boswell's (25).

Figure 6.3. Doorframe of the Condon Vault Entrance. The vault doorframe is now used as an exit in the Dalton Defenders Museum.

Once the Condon cash from the counter and the money drawer was in the sack, Grat asked for any other currency and the gold. He ordered Ball and Carpenter into the vault, and, as they turned to enter, he discovered Babb. Grat cursed the young bookkeeper and told him to come out from behind the book rack with his hands up.

In the vault the doors of the safe were standing open, though a combination lock was visible on a closed burglar-proof chest. Three canvas bags containing silver were visible in the safe, and Grat ordered Carpenter to empty these into the sack Ball was holding. Carpenter complied, so $3,000 in silver dollars went into the sack, making it weigh about 200 pounds.

Grat then ordered Ball to open the burglar-proof chest, but Ball said that it was on a time-lock setting and could not be opened until 9:30. (Actually the time-lock had been set for 8:00 A.M., and it had gone off at that time.) Grat asked, "What time is it now?" (*Last Raid* 30) Ball, glancing at his watch, said 9:20 (although it was really 9:40.) Carpenter wrote, "Had Grat looked at the clock on the wall he might have seen for himself" (25). Grat said—fateful statement—"We can wait" (*Last Raid* 30).[6]

Ball had made up the time-setting ploy because the chest contained over $40,000. He had made a quick guess as to the current time. It was then actually 9:40 A.M. Carpenter helped with the ruse by turning the chest handle to show it was locked. Grat, impatient, finally said he thought they were lying. He demanded to see their gold.

When Ball said they had no gold, Grat asked how much cash the bank's books had shown the previous evening. Ball replied $4,000: $1,000 in currency and $3,000 in silver, all of which was now in the sack. Ball went on to say that there was nothing in the chest with the time-lock except small change; the bank had ordered some currency, but it had not yet arrived.

While that was going on in the Condon, Bob and Emmett Dalton, in the First National Bank, were having better luck, though they too had no idea that the alarm had been given. When Bob and Emmett had entered, three customers—J. H. Brewster, A. W. Knotts, and C. L. Hollingsworth—were in the bank. Jim E. S. Boothby, another customer, had stepped into the bank a moment or two after the robbers. Seeing what was going on, he started to back out of the bank; one of the Daltons, waving his rifle, motioned him inside.

Cashier Thomas G. Ayres and W. H. Shepard, the teller, had been in the front of the bank behind the counter, Ayres at the cashier's window and the teller at his desk near the vault. Leaving Emmett on guard in this front area of the bank, Bob went through a hall into the private office in the rear of the bank, where Bert S. Ayres, the young bookkeeper, was at his desk. This private office also had a door opening into a vacant lot that gave access to the alley which ran north and south at the rear of the bank.

Bob ordered Ayres to go to the front of the bank where the vault was located and to hand over the money. When Ayres didn't move quickly enough, both Daltons swore at him and threatened to shoot him. The bookkeeper handed over the money on the counter and that in the cash drawer; then Bob ordered him to get the money from the safe. The bookkeeper said that he did not know the combination.

Cashier Ayres went to the safe and returned with some money, which he put in the grain sack the Daltons had carried in with them. Bob asked if they now had all the money. The Cashier said there was still some gold in the vault and asked if they also wanted that. Bob answered yes, that they wanted every cent.

The Cashier then went back to the vault and returned with the gold. Bob again asked if that was all. Ayres said it was and pushed the safe door shut. Bob, obviously not convinced, entered the vault, opened the safe door and removed two more packages of money, each containing $5,000. Angrily, Bob threw these packages into the money sack, which now contained about $21,000. Bob next swept some silver that was in the vault onto the floor. He picked up a box containing some gold watches, but, when the bank employees said that box held nothing but papers, he put it down.

Figure 6.4. The First National Bank Safe

Making the three bank employees go out in front of the counter, Bob and Emmett ordered the three bankers and the four customers to leave by the front door.

Rammel Brothers Drug adjoined the First National Bank on the north. Just as the bank personnel and the bank customers reached the sidewalk, George Cubine, with his Winchester, and American Express agent C. S. Cox, with a revolver, fired from the doorway of the drug store at Bob and Emmett in the front door of the First National. Neither shot hit the Daltons, but they jumped back into the bank. Two of the bank employees, Bert Ayres and Shepard, also retreated into the comparative safety of the bank building. Cashier Ayres ran out the front door of the bank and into Isham's. There he grabbed a rifle and moved to stand in the north door of the hardware store, from which he had a good view north to the door of the First National.

At this point some of the citizen defenders opened fire on the Condon, shattering the plate glass windows. One who fired was Parker Williams, from his vantage point on Barndollar's awning. Broadwell, standing at the southeast entrance of the Condon, put his Winchester against the plate glass in the door and fired at Williams, but missed. Broadwell's second shot, fired through the hole made by the first, went through an open window on the second floor of the Barndollar store and lodged in some queensware stored on the shelves. Williams eventually left the awning, but not before seeing Broadwell drop his Winchester and grab his right arm.[7]

Still in the First National, Bob moved back to the bank front door while Emmett, holding his Winchester under one arm, tied a string around the opening of the money sack. Bob took aim and fired. His shot hit Charles Gump, who was still standing by Isham's awning post.[8] The bullet first struck Gump on his gun hand and then went on to strike his gun. The shotgun fell in pieces on the sidewalk, and friends helped the wounded man back into Isham's.

The third Isham employee, Reynolds, taking the rifle he had grabbed from inventory, ran out onto the sidewalk and began shooting west toward Broadwell at the southeast door of the Condon. A shot from that outlaw's rifle glanced off something and then struck

Reynolds at the base of the little toe on his right foot, coming out his instep. Friends helped him back into Isham's too.[9]

Bob and Emmett then told Shepard to open the back door of the First National for them, and they moved toward that door. At about the same time, Lucius M. Baldwin went out the back door of Isham's into the alley. He reached the alley just as Bob and Emmett came to the rear door of the First National Bank, with Shepard accompanying them. Shepard opened the door and the Daltons came out.

Baldwin, holding the pistol down at his side, started forward. The young clerk looked as if he planned to join the three men at the back of the bank, probably thinking they were armed citizens. Both Bob and Emmett leveled their rifles at him and ordered him to stop. Either not hearing the order or not understanding it, Baldwin moved further toward them, until he was about 50 feet away. Bob raised his rifle and fired. The bullet hit Baldwin in the left chest and passed through his body. The Daltons turned and ran toward the north entrance of the alley where it opened onto Eighth Street. Baldwin also was carried into Isham's. There were now three wounded citizens in Isham's, all bleeding profusely. Though Baldwin lived until the next day, his wound was fatal.

Emmett, carrying the money sack, ran in front of Bob, who kept his rifle at the ready. When they reached Eighth Street, they turned west toward Union. At the corner of Union and Eighth, they glanced south and fired two shots in that direction.

M. N. Anderson, a carpenter working a couple of blocks away, had hurried to Isham's when he'd learned of the excitement. Anderson picked up the rifle Reynolds had been holding and stood near the door, beside Henry Isham. Charles K. Smith, from **Smith's Barber Shop**, also got a rifle from the shelves and joined the other defenders in the store.[10] At this point each of the defenders had fired from five to nine shots at the outlaws.

In the Condon, Power and Broadwell had also been busy, each firing from four to six times at citizens outside the bank. Grat asked if there was a back door through which they could leave, but he was told there was not.[11] He then told Ball and Carpenter to carry the sack of money to the front door. When the two bank employees and Grat reached the area outside of the counter, so many shots were coming through the windows that the three robbers and the bankers all retreated behind the counter. The bankers and the two customers stretched out on the floor to avoid the bullets that flew everywhere as the citizens in front of Boswell's fired about 80 shots into the bank.

At this point Power was heard to say that he'd been hit and couldn't use his arm, that he couldn't shoot any longer. Grat then ordered Ball to open the sack and give him only the currency. Ball, emptying the sack on the floor, heard a bullet from outside pass close to his head; he hurriedly handed the currency over to Grat, who stuffed it in his vest.

Bob and Emmett were continuing west on Eighth, having reached the middle of the intersection of Eighth and Union. From there they could see Cubine, with his Winchester ready, standing in the doorway of Rammel's, looking south toward the First National. Four shots were fired from the intersection, about 40 or 50 yards away, and Cubine fell dead, shot in the back. He had one bullet through his heart, one in his thigh and a third in an ankle. The fourth bullet went through the plate glass window of the drug store.

Charles Brown, an elderly shoemaker, approached Cubine's body. Seeing that his fellow citizen was dead, the unarmed Brown picked up Cubine's gun and turned toward the Daltons. Four more shots were fired from the intersection, and Brown, a Civil War veteran, fell within two feet of Cubine. Although he lived for a few hours, Brown's wound would also prove fatal.

At about the time Bob and Emmett reached Eighth Street, Grat, in the Condon, finished stuffing the money into his vest and ran out the Condon's southwest door and headed for the alley, his companions following. Grat fired two shots as he ran out. Outside the Condon, Grat, Power, and Broadwell found themselves caught in a crossfire between the men at Isham's and the men on the south side of the plaza in front of Boswell's.

As their partners were leaving the Condon, Bob and Emmett finished crossing Union at Eighth and began mounting the steps to the raised sidewalk at the corner. Seeing Thomas Ayres in the north door of Isham's, Bob took careful aim, and, from about 75 yards away, fired. The bullet entered below Ayres's left eye and came out at the base of his skull. George Picker quickly pressed his thumb over Ayres's spouting blood, undoubtedly saving his life (Carpenter 26).

Just as Ayres fell, Grat and his two companions from the Condon reached the alley opening. Before Ayres could even be pulled to safety, the fleeing gang fired nine shots into Isham's.

Bob and Emmett, leaving the corner of Eighth and Union, continued west on Eighth. They were not seen again until they appeared at the junction of the two alleys dividing block 50.

As Emmett and Bob turned left from Eighth into the north/south alley, they ran into 14 year-old Robert L. Wells Jr., who was holding a .22 pistol. One of the outlaws tapped the lad with his rifle; the other cursed at him and told him to run home or he was liable to get hurt. Elliott wrote, "The boy was not slow in obeying the command" (*Last Raid* 64).

Notes to Chapter 6: The Raid

1   Versions differ about who gave the first alarm. Jacob Thomas Perry, a young employee of the **Suthard and Blease Boot and Shoe Shop**, wrote his memories of the raid some sixty-five years later. He said that Charley Smith, who was with Smith's Barber Shop just south of Isham's, spread the news to the men at Isham's and Boswell's (3D).

Sixty years later, returning to Coffeyville for a visit, J. P. Moran, who had been the driver of the oil tank parked in the alley, said he believed he was the one who gave the first alarm. "When I told Bert Florea and Harry Lang, clerks in Slosson's Drug Store, that the banks were being robbed, they just laughed at me" ("Daltons!" 2D). Moran was undoubtedly mistaken about his alarm's being the first, however, as he said that Lang, when he saw that a robbery actually was in progress, grabbed a shotgun and fired the first shot at the robbers. Based on the known sequence of events, other citizens were aware of the robberies by the time the first shot was fired.

Emmett wrote that Charles Gump alerted the citizenry. Emmett also said that Bob fired at Gump to prevent his giving the alarm, wounding him in the hand (*When the Daltons Rode* 240). This is definitely incorrect. Gump was not wounded until after the outlaws had left the banks, and the alarm was given before that. Gump believed he was the first to give the alarm, but said that Bob did not fire at him at that time (Latta 221).

2   Latta believed that the Coffeyville citizens had been warned. He used a 1942 letter from, and an 1944 interview with, Ex-Deputy U. S. Marshal George A. Yoes as evidence. A portion of Yoes's statement follows: "I am the only man living who knows just how they got put out of business. I have never before told anyone about it, but here is the story" (224).

Yoes went on to say that an outlaw who had been in jail in Ft. Smith had told him that the Daltons were going to rob two banks—either in Van Buren, Arkansas, or in Coffeyville. Yoes said that he and other lawmen armed the merchants at Van Buren and "notified the banks at Coffeyville" (224).

Latta also quoted a letter from Chris Madsen written after Yoes's account was released. Madsen agreed that U.S. Marshal Jacob Yoes (the father of George Yoes) notified the

U.S. marshal at Guthrie, Oklahoma, that the Dalton gang was planning to rob banks at either Van Buren, Arkansas, or Coffeyville. Madsen's letter, however, did not say that the banks were notified.

> I notified the deputies near the Oklahoma and Kansas borders to be prepared to take the field at once if ordered by wire. As some of the deputies were too talkative, I did not let them know what information we had from Mr. Yoes.... we kept our office open day and night, waiting for news. (225-26)

In most cases I found Latta's book to be a most helpful resource, but this story from Yoes, not told until fifty-two years later, seems highly unlikely. (Also I tend to be suspicious when a person says he or she is the only person living who knows some particular information.) If the Coffeyville banks were forewarned, why didn't any of the bank officers or employees have guns? Why wasn't Marshal Connelly armed? Why were women and children, one of them Elliott's own daughter, milling around the plaza the morning of the raid if the townspeople had been warned to expect the Daltons? ("Too Excited")

3   Elliott, on page 37 of Last Raid, wrote that Isham's was north of the First National Bank. This was most certainly an error that was missed in proofreading, as all his other mentions of direction in terms of that store correctly placed it south of the bank.

4   The mention of only one customer came from Elliott's account in the October 7, 1892, Journal. In Last Raid, after he'd had time to talk to more of the townspeople involved, Elliott wrote that two customers had entered the Condon; the second customer was D. E. James. Two was probably the correct number, as Carpenter, who was in the bank, also mentioned the two customers by name (25).

5   Carpenter remembered that Grat gave the sack directly to him (24).

6   Elliott's account in the October 7, 1892, Journal indicated that the wait would be three minutes. In Last Raid he indicated that it would be ten. The issue of any delay, however short, was the important one.

7   Elliott's contemporary accounts disagreed a bit at this point. In the October 7, 1892, Journal, he stated that Williams was on

Barndollar's awning. In *Last Raid*, Elliott said that Williams climbed on Boswell's awning. The picture of Boswell's included in Last Raid, however, showed no awning attached to its front. Since a contemporary picture of the Union side of the plaza showed an awning in front of Barndollar Brothers, it seems safe to assume that Williams was firing from the awning over the front of the Barndollar store.

8   Gump said he had thought Emmett was the one who shot him as the outlaws started to leave the front door of the First National Bank. Gump changed his mind after Emmett later told him that Bob had been the one who shot him (Latta 221-22).

9   Carpenter thought that Lew Dietz, the other Isham's employee, was also wounded (26).

10 Elliott said that Charles K. Smith was the son of the proprietor of the barber shop. Perry said that Charley Smith, who gave the alarm, was with the Smith Barber Shop. Therefore the defender with the rifle was probably the citizen who had given the alarm on the east side of the plaza.

11 This was a second ruse, as Cashier Ball's office did have a door opening onto Walnut.

Chapter 7: The Alley

Elliott's book, *Last Raid of the Daltons*, published in 1892, and his newspaper account of the raid published on October 7, 1892, are also the principal sources for this chapter. Again, because of the brevity of these works, individual page numbers are cited only for direct quotes. Any other sources used are indicated in the text.

As occurs elsewhere, the locations printed in boldface type at their first mention can be found in *Figure 5.1. Map of the Plaza Area in 1892*.

When Grat, Broadwell, and Power left the Condon, they ran directly into the line of fire from both the men at Isham's and those at Boswell's. Grat and Power received serious wounds before they had retreated twenty steps. Finally the outlaws from the Condon made it to the east/west alley and were lost to the sight of the men at Boswell's. The men near Isham's still had a relatively good field of fire.

Power tried to take refuge in the rear door of a store, but the door was locked. Clinging his rifle, he staggered west down the alley to his horse. Then another shot hit him in the back, and he fell dead beside his horse.

Grat, using the cover of the oil tank, reached the stable west of the jail. The guns from Isham's could not reach him there because an outside stairway on Slosson's jutted out into the alley. Grat stood by the stable a few minutes, firing several wild shots. One even thudded into a door frame close to several citizens standing on the south side of Ninth Street.

John Kloehr, Carey A. Seamen—a barber—and Marshal Charles T. Connelly were on the south side of the plaza near Read's when the gang reached the alley. They started west on Ninth to intercept the outlaws before they could get to their horses.

As they hurried west, Connelly said he needed to get a gun. The Marshal ran into the **Swisher Brothers Machine Shop**, a short distance west on Ninth, and borrowed a rifle. He then hurried across the vacant lot on the north side of Ninth to an opening in the fence. He entered the alley at the west corner of the stable where Grat was standing. The Marshal came into the alley looking west, toward the outlaws' horses. This action placed his back toward Grat, who raised his rifle to his side and fired without taking aim. Connelly fell forward, dying just as the fight ended.

Grat then tried again to reach his horse. He passed the Marshal's body and turned to face his attackers, trying to use his rifle. Kloehr fired another shot, which hit Grat in the throat and broke his neck.

Meanwhile Dick Broadwell, though wounded, had reached cover in the Long-Bell Lumber Company's yard. Because their rearing disturbed his aim, he shot the two horses harnessed to the oil tank (Carpenter 26). A lull occurred after Grat and Power fell, so Broadwell crawled out of hiding, mounted his horse, and rode away. A bullet from Kloehr's rifle and a load of shot from Seaman's shotgun hit him. Bleeding and dying, he hung on to his horse and managed to get away from the fight scene.

At about the time that the three outlaws from the Condon reached the east/west alley, Bob and Emmett were running south from Eighth Street through the alley that divided the north half of block 50. Near the junction of the two alleys, they saw F. D. Benson climbing through a rear window of Slosson & Co's drug store. Bob fired at him, but his bullet hit the window.

Bob then stepped out into the east/west alley, glancing up toward the tops of the surrounding buildings as if he thought the shots he could hear being fired might be coming from the rooftops. As Bob stepped out, he was visible to the men at Isham's, who fired. Hit, Bob staggered across the alley and sat down on a pile of curbstones stacked near the jail. While sitting there, he fired several times, but the bullets went wild.[1]

Bob spotted John Kloehr inside the fence at the back of his livery business. Bob tried to raise his rifle to his shoulder but could not get it up to aim. His shot went wide. Bob managed to stand and move to the stable west of the jail where, leaning against the corner, he fired two more shots. A shot from Kloehr's rifle then struck Bob in the chest, and he fell to the ground.[2]

Emmett, still carrying the grain sack with approximately $21,000 of the First National Bank's money, had managed to escape unhurt up to this time. The horses belonging to Bob and Power had been between Emmett and the defenders; both horses were killed by shots intended for Emmett. Finally he reached his horse. A half-dozen shots went in his direction as he attempted to mount. Wounded in the right arm and in the left hip and groin, Emmett managed to get in his saddle.

All accounts agree that Emmett, still clinging to the sack containing the First National money, chose not to ride away. Instead, he rode back to where Bob was lying, reached down his hand, and tried to lift his dying or dead brother onto the horse with him. Elliott's account said Bob whispered, "It's no use" (*Last Raid* 55). Then Seaman fired both barrels of his shotgun at Emmett's back, and he fell from the horse.

At last came the cry: "They are all down!" ("Daltons!" 1).

Notes to Chapter 7: The Alley

1 Carpenter wrote that Henry Isham shot Bob through the heart and that the leader of the Daltons was dead when he fell (26).

2 Kloehr's sister Mary was at her brother's side during the battle. She said that Kloehr was dismayed at killing Bob, as the two had been friends ("John J. Kloehr").

Chapter 8: The Aftermath

Elliott's book, *Last Raid of the Daltons*, published in 1892, and his newspaper account of the raid published on October 7, 1892, are also important sources for this chapter. As has been the case earlier, because of the brevity of these works, individual page numbers are cited only for direct quotes. Other sources used are indicated in the text.

As was true in the two preceding chapters, those locations printed in boldface type at their first mention can be found in *Figure 5.1. Map of the Plaza Area in 1892.*

A hush fell with the last shotgun blast. In the alley three men lay dead, a fourth was dying, and Emmett was bleeding and helpless. The entire gunfight had lasted less than fifteen minutes, but bodies, dead horses, and smoking rifles seemed to be everywhere. Then some of the defending citizens hurried to those who had fallen.

Bob was dead by the time the first man reached him. His rifle was empty, but the revolver in his belt had not been fired.[1] He also had a revolver in his boot and another in his vest pocket.

Power's Winchester was empty too. He had neither money nor identification on his body.

Grat still had his false whiskers on his face. The currency from the Condon, nearly $1,100, remained stuffed inside his vest. His rifle was lying by his side, but his two Colt revolvers had not been fired.

Elliott was the first to reach Emmett ("Working"). The youngest Dalton, who had fallen with his rifle in his hand, held up his uninjured hand in surrender.[2] Elliott disarmed Emmett, picking up his revolvers and setting his rifle aside. The two loaded revolvers had not been fired. H. W. Read gathered up the burlap grain bag of money lying near Emmett and carried it to the bank ("Read's Began").

A man ran from the **Farmer's Home Boarding House** carrying a rope. The sight of the rope aroused the crowd, and soon there were many who wanted to lynch Emmett. Dr. Walter H. Wells protested, saying that the outlaw was so severely wounded that they might as well hang a dead man. Emmett was finally carried into Slosson's drug and then upstairs to **Dr. Wells's office**. There the doctor treated the young outlaw's wounds, removing twenty-three slugs from his body. Later Emmett was carried to a room at the Farmer's Home and closely guarded.[3]

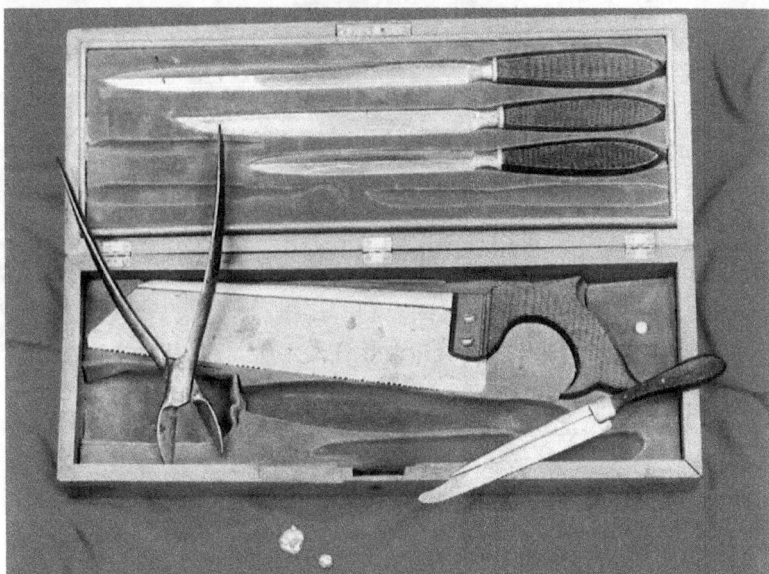

Figure 8.1. Instruments belonging to Dr. W. H. Wells

Marshal Connelly was also carried into Slosson's, but he was dead by the time he was examined.

After Emmett and the Marshal had been carried from the alley, a rack for loose hay was placed against the stable on the south side of the alley. Boards were carried from the Long-Bell Lumber Company yard and propped against the hay rack ("Family Prompted" 3D). The bodies of Grat, Bob, and Power were stretched out on the boards.

Figure 8.2. Death Alley after the Raid: This photo looks west from between Slosson Drug on the left and McKenna and Adamson's on the right. The jail is the small white stone building on the left about three doors beyond Slosson's. The frame building beyond the jail is the stable. The north/south alley opens onto the one on the lower right, where a group of people are gathered.

Figure 8.3. A Closer View of Death Alley

Then reaction set in. Coffeyville was in shock. Eight men had just died, and four others had been wounded. Townsmen Lucius M. Baldwin, George B. Cubine, Charles Brown, and Marshall Connelly had been killed by the outlaws. Three other townsmen had been wounded: Charles T. Gump, T. Arthur Reynolds, and Thomas Ayres. Of the outlaws, Bob and Grat Dalton, Dick Broadwell, and Bill Power were dead; Emmett was severely wounded.

> Business was suspended and an extra detail of police put on duty. Knots of excited man gathered at every convenient point, and the dreadful occurrences of the day were discussed. The afternoon and evening trains brought hundreds of visitors from adjoining towns. (Elliott "Daltons!" 5)

Superintendent Frey of the Katy and about fifty armed men arrived from Parsons by train, making the 45 mile trip in thirty-two minutes in response to a telegram sent during the raid. Other telegrams arrived offering additional assistance. *Journal* Editor Elliott received seventeen telegrams within two hours of the raid, one of which was from a *New York Herald* official.

Both sightseers and citizens thronged the alley and the plaza area. Some took small pieces of the gang's clothing for souvenirs. The four bodies were photographed and eventually put into the city jail overnight.

Figure 8.4. The Dalton Gang: four Dead, one alive: The boards holding the dead outlaws are leaning up against the alley side of the stable. From left to right, the dead outlaws are Bill Power, Bob Dalton, Grat Dalton, and Dick Broadwell. Emmett's picture is inserted at the upper left.

On Thursday the banks tried to reconcile their balances. The First National showed a positive balance of \$1.98, while the Condon showed the bank was missing \$20.00 after the raid. That afternoon U.S. Marshal Payne of Oklahoma arrived to get a look at the remains of the Dalton gang. He claimed he had been following them for fifteen months.[4]

Both Coffeyville and Independence were eager to get the legal process against Emmett underway. H. M. Stansbury, William McCoy, Luther Perkins, D. Stewart Elliott, J. E. S. Boothby, J. H. Brewster, W. R. Cubine, and James Evans appeared before Coffeyville Justice of the Peace C. L. Long on Thursday to swear out a complaint against Emmett. Long issued two warrants: one for Emmett's arrest for Baldwin's murder and a second for his arrest for Cubine's. William Kime, Coffeyville Constable, then officially arrested Emmett. Long read the complaint and warrants to Emmett and asked if he were ready to proceed with a preliminary hearing. Emmett wanted to waive his right to that hearing, but Long admonished him to "procure council before makeing answer [sic]" (*Case File #7257*).

On that same day in Independence, F. J. Fritch (who was later to be appointed Emmett's defense attorney) swore out a complaint before Justice of the Peace G. E. Gilmore. Fritch's complaint charged that Emmett had murdered Lucius Baldwin.[5] Gilmore immediately issued a warrant for Emmett's arrest for that murder (*Case File #7257*).

Then the city went into mourning over the death of Marshal Connelly, George Cubine, Charley Brown and Lucius Baldwin. Stalwart men wept great tears of grief, whilst the women and children cried and wrung their hands in agony. (Elliott "Daltons!" 5)

The next day George Cubine was buried in Elmwood Cemetery. His widow and a seven-year-old son survived the 36-year-old Cubine. Two other children had died in infancy. ("In Memoriam"). That same afternoon **Lang and Lape Undertakers** buried the two Daltons and

Power in black-varnished coffins, also in Elmwood Cemetery.

Figure 8.5. Bob's Boot Gun and Burial Records

On Friday, Ben and Bill Dalton, with their mother and sister, Mrs. Whipple (Eva), arrived from Kingfisher, Oklahoma.[6] Broadwell's brother and brother-in-law (both from good families in Hutchinson) arrived and identified their relative, who had sometimes been known as John Moore or Texas Jack. His body was put in a sealed can for future shipment to Hutchinson. No friend or relative of Bill Power was heard from.

Friday was also the day Marshal Connelly was buried in the Independence cemetery. Connelly, 46, was survived by two grown children from his first marriage—a son and a daughter, and by his second wife and a minor daughter ("In Memoriam"). Also that day a memorial service was held for Lucius Baldwin in

Burlington, Kansas. Baldwin, who was 23, was survived by his mother ("Obituary").

Figure 8.6. Marshall Connelly's Gun with Mementoes

Figure 8.7. Burlap Money Sack with Gun Baldwin Carried

At least 2,000 people had visited Coffeyville by Friday evening. During the next few days, trains brought hundreds more visitors. Souvenir hunters cut portions from the manes and tails of the Dalton horses and cut all the strings from their saddles.

Charles Brown's funeral was held on Saturday afternoon in Coffeyville. Brown, 59, was survived by his wife, who was referred to as "an aged widow in dependent circumstances" ("Obituary").

Adeline Dalton and all the family except Bill left for home after a few days. She and Ben sent a note to the *Journal* expressing their thanks to Dr. Wells and to other citizens for their kind treatment, saying "We have no enmity against any one whatever on account of the late terrible tragedy" ("A Card").

Sheriff Callahan had planned to move Emmett to the jail at Independence on Friday, but decided against it. He was afraid the outlaw would be lynched if he removed him from the room where he'd been confined at the Farmer's Home. By the next Tuesday, October 11th, the sheriff apparently considered it safe, for Emmett was transported to Independence and brought before Justice of the Peace Gilmore. Emmett waived a preliminary examination and was ordered "Committed to the Jail of Montgomery County until discharged according to law" (*Case File #7257*).

Bill Dalton stuck around and began making protests about the town's treatment of his brothers and their possessions. He claimed that Bob had had about $900 with him at the time of the robbery, and that the money was missing. He also said that Emmett's guns and his horse should be returned to him.

Compassion for Emmett began to surface. Two Independence papers, the *Reporter* and the *Star and Kansan*, expressed sympathy for Emmett. So did at least one Kansas congressman. A letter appeared in the

Kansas City Journal stating that Congressman Jerry Simpson had said,

> The Dalton boys were no worse than the national bankers and thousands of others in Kansas who are engaged in pretended lawful pursuits, while really they are robbing the people. They are to be no more condemned for their acts than the bankers they robbed. (Samuelson *Story* 121)[7]

On December 2, Elliott was served with a writ of replevin demanding that he give up Emmett's guns. Angry, Elliott turned the guns over to the constable, but maintained Emmett had "surrendered" the guns to him in the alley ("Working Their Scheme").

An article in *The Journal* quoted the *Independence Reporter*. The Independence paper accused Elliott of stealing Emmett's guns, then continued "We do not believe that ravings of D. Stewart Elliott... represent the feelings of the citizens of Coffeyville, and the sooner they have their wind shut off the better" ("Our Friends").

Elliott furiously replied that four Coffeyville citizens had already had their wind shut off. "Coffeyville has suffered enough, too much, from this gang already. There will be no shutting off of wind" ("Our Friends"). He went on to write:

> ...the public ought to know that every man who had anything to do with wiping out the raiders is spotted; that threats have been made openly and covertly, against the defenders of Coffeyville's honor and property of her citizens; that armed allies of the Dalton's [sic] frequent

> our city and by their presence threaten the
> personal safety of the heroes who flew to
> the defense of right on the 5th of October.
> ("A Human Hyena")

Coffeyville citizens were worrying about rebuttal from outlaws who might have worked with the Dalton gang. When a train was held up outside of nearby Caney, Kansas, on October 12, rumors of Dalton gang survivors spread rapidly ("More Robbers!"). Kate Read, in a sympathy letter to Lucius Baldwin's mother dated October 15, 1892, wrote "We have been warned of another raid by the Dalton gang and the people are armed and try to be ready. There are over fifty Winchesters in readiness... I am frightened all the time" (Green 10).

According to a letter Marshal Tibbils wrote to Elliott, John Kloehr had apparently received a threatening letter purporting to be from remnants of the gang. Tibbils sought to reassure Coffeyville citizens that the Dalton gang was no more. The Marshal closed by saying,

> Sincerely hoping that the people of
> Coffeyville may at once become quieted
> and their peace of mind restored and that
> Coffeyville will ever retain the proud
> distinction that she will never want for
> brave and true men to guard her wealth
> and the lives of her people.

Some newspapers wanted to blame the cheap literature of the day for attracting the Daltons and others to a life of crime. The *Topeka State Journal* said that Jesse James, for example, had been written up in ways that made him seem a hero. The *Kansas City Journal* wrote:

There ought to be a lesson in these all too frequently [sic] tragedies that should put a stop to the public education of the ignorant and brutally disposed in the sentiment of outlawry. The main source of the evil is found on every news stand... ("Dalton Raid").

Most newspapers were full of praise for Coffeyville's citizens. The *Liberty Review* wrote "Perhaps no other city in Kansas could have made the fight against a gang of desperadoes that Coffeyville did" ("Dalton Raid"). The *Topeka Capital* wrote:

Nothing has taken hold so powerfully of the sympathy and admiration of the country for a long time, as the heroic conduct of Marshal Connelly, Liveryman Kloehr and their little body of associates at Coffeyville on the occasion of the last sortie of the Dalton gang. From every state in the Union have come words of admiration for the superb courage and steady nerve of Coffeyville's intrepid citizens. ("Dalton Raid")

The *Washington Post* pointed out that the citizen defenders came from every walk of life and continued:

What this country needs is a multiplication of Coffeyvilles. Towns of that caliber should be distributed freely all over this glorious and happy land. Wherever robbers, murderers, incendiaries and bandits congregate, some new Coffeyville should spring up in the night, populated by Browns, Connellys, Kloehrs,

Baldwins and Cubines, and filled with a spirit of emulation in marksmanship. No county in any State should be without its Coffeyville. ("Dalton Raid")

Fame came to those citizens who had successfully defended their town. Much of this fame centered around John Kloehr, who was credited with killing Bob and Grat Dalton and Dick Broadwell, and with wounding Emmett. Seeing his friend Connelly shot in the back had spurred Kloehr to action.

Soon after the raid, when a stranger asked Kloehr for his name, the modest defender, not craving publicity, replied "Jim Spears." The stranger turned out to be a representative of the Winchester arms company. Not long afterwards Kloehr received a rifle from that company bearing the following inscription: "Jim Spears, Coffeyville, Kansas, compliments of the Winchester Repeating Arms company" ("John J. Kloehr").

The rifle was not the only gift sent by those wanting to honor sharpshooter Kloehr. A boot company offered "to send him a fine pair of hunting boots" ("Tid-Bits from the Telegram"). The *Kansas City Star* suggested running him for governor in 1894 ("Dalton Raid").

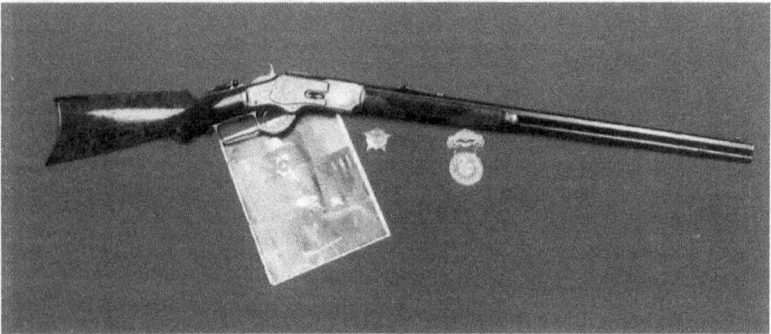

Figure 8.8. Kloehr's Picture, Medal, Badge, and Gun

The citizens of Chicago sent Kloehr a gold medal with a diamond in the center. On the front of the medal was inscribed "John Joseph Kloehr: The Emergency Arose, The Man Appeared." On the back were the words "Presented by friends in Chicago who admire nerve and courage when displayed in defense of social order."

Figure 8.9. A Close-up of the Medal

In the following portion of his letter to the Chicago citizens, thanking them for the impressive medal, Kloehr effectively demonstrated the kind of man he was.

> I take pleasure in accepting [the medal] as a token of your appreciation of an act accomplished only in the performance of a citizen's duty in defending the best I could the interest of the city and my friends, and upholding the law, as I think every citizen should,... whatever may have been the result of my work, it was not due to my having any more courage than many of my neighbors whose names have not been heralded over this great nation of ours as has mine.
>
> I value this magnificent emblem of your approval and good will beyond expression, and I shall treasure it as emblematic of the fact that the world likes a man who does his duty well. (Kloehr)

The citizens of Coffeyville had rallied when the need arose to defend their banks. They rallied again on the second day following the raid, this time to come to the aid of the families of the dead defenders. In a mass meeting the citizens resolved to begin collecting money for the families. A circular was prepared and sent out appealing to financial institutions, railroads, and express companies ("Citizens Meet").

On October 21, 1892, the Relief Committee had already received $5,275 in donations. By December 2nd, $12,000 had been distributed to the families. Baldwin's mother and the widows of Cubine, Brown, and Connelly each received $1,650. Cubine's elderly mother received $100. Connelly's older daughter received $680. Set aside in trust for Connelly's minor daughter was $1,140;

$1,440 was also set aside for Cubine's minor son. To help with expenses while the defenders recovered from their wounds, the committee awarded $1,200 to Charles Gump and $840 to T. A. Reynolds, Gump getting the larger amount since his injuries were permanent ("Relief Committee Meeting"). There is no mention of an allotment to banker Ayres, which may indicate that he declined any financial assistance.

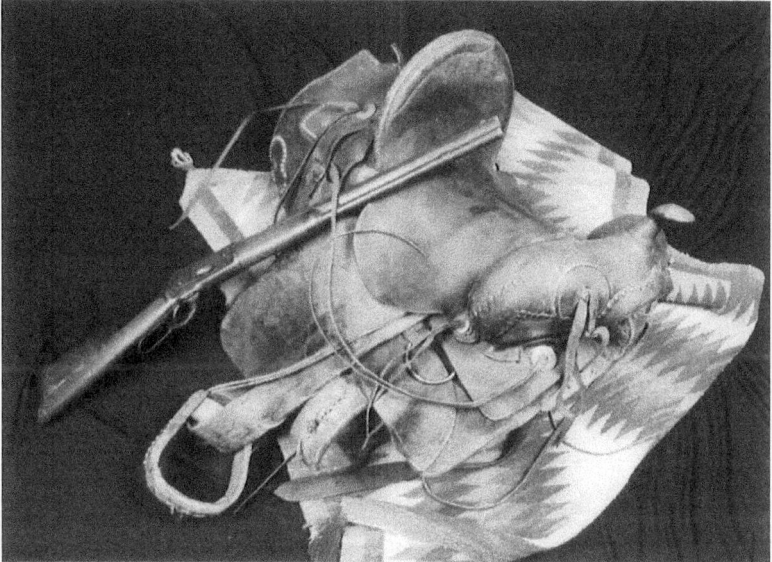

Figure 8.10. Bob's Saddle with Grat's Rifle

Sheriff John Callahan was named the administrator of Bob's and Grat's estates. The list of assets in Bob's estate included $900 in cash, in addition to his saddle, rifle, and six-shooters, so Bill had obviously been correct about the amount of cash Bob had been carrying the morning of the raid (Samuelson *Story* 127). In January 1893 Sheriff Callahan auctioned off Bob's and Grat's guns, saddles, and other personal belongings with them at the time of the raid. Quite a few people turned up to bid on the various items. John Kloehr purchased Grat's horse for $90 and Bob's saddle for $23.50. W. H. Clark purchased one of Bob's revolvers for $31.00. The total earned from the auction, $294.25, was applied toward the Daltons' debts (*Coffeyville at 100* 27).

Figure 8.11. Bob's Pearl-Handled Revolver with Cartridge Belt and Oil Can

Figure 8.12. Bob's Vest-Pocket .38 Caliber British Bulldog

On December 14th, J. R. Charlton, Montgomery County attorney, filed a complaint against Emmett with Justice of the Peace Gilmore of Independence for the murder of George Cubine during the robbery of the First National Bank.[8] Gilmore issued a justice's warrant to Sheriff Callahan, requiring him to bring Emmett before the court "to be dealt with according to law." Emmett's case was then "by agreement continued" to December 16th (*Case File #7287*).

On the 16th Charlton swore out two district court complaints: one against Emmett for the murder of Lucius Baldwin during the First National robbery (this complaint listed thirty-nine witnesses) and a second against Emmett for the murder of Cubine (*Case File #7287*). Emmett, represented by attorney F. J. Fritch, appeared and "demanded an examination." Emmett's hearing was then scheduled for January 16, 1893, at 9:00 A. M. (*Case File #7287*).[9]

At the January 16th hearing in Montgomery County, again presided over by Justice of the Peace Gilmore, attorneys W. E. Zeigler and J. R. Charlton represented the state and attorney F. J. Fritch represented Emmett. The transcript showed that there were two complaints and warrants pending against Emmett.

> Deft [defendant] files motion to quash proceeding under this complaint and warrant for the reason that there is now pending in District Court in and for Montgomery County Kansas all information against the defendant charging him with the same offense and proceeding against him for the same unlawful act as that charged in said complaint and warrant in this action. (*Case File #7287*)

Both this motion to quash, and an objection to any introduction of evidence because of the reasons cited in the motion to quash, were overruled. The transcript reported that L. G. Ayres, T. H. Brooks, William McCoy, and Kirby Long testified before the State rested. "Defendant [did] not introduce any evidence and refused to cross examine witnesses" (*Case File #7287*). Emmett was sent back to jail to wait for trial during the next district court term, which would be in March.[10]

Emmett's March trial had a standing-room-only crowd. Many Coffeyville citizens made the trip to Independence to hear Emmett's testimony and the testimony of their friends and relatives who had been on or near the plaza at the time of the raid. The following were subpoenaed to appear:

> Thomas G. Ayres, W. H. Shepard, Ed Jackson, D. S. Elliott, W. T. Dean, Kirby Long, William McCoy, William Myers, C. S. Cox, Dick Fulkerson, John J. Kloehr, Joseph Johnson, Harry Hines, R. P. Kerchival, J. K. Morgan, Jacob Staats, William Mack, H. W. Reed, Mrs. H. W. Reed, Mrs. E. J Hines, Mrs. Lee Tally, T. J. Dodge, T. H. Brooks, and Joseph Savage. (*Case File # 7287*)

Throughout the preceding months Emmett had maintained that he had shot no one during the raid, that Cubine and Baldwin were killed by Bob. As his trial began on March 7, 1893, Emmett pleaded "not guilty." In *When the Daltons Rode*, written forty-four years later, Emmett discussed his plea:

> My attorney, Joseph Fritch, felt assured that if I pleaded guilty to second-degree killing in the Cubine case the other

charges would be dismissed. He also felt reasonably certain that I would get close to the minimum sentence, perhaps ten to fifteen years. (267)

Emmett was persuaded to change his plea. The March 8th court records showed that the defendant withdrew his plea of "not guilty" and entered a plea of "guilty of murder in the second degree" (*Trial Docket*).

Figure 8.13. Judge McCue's Desk, Grat's Rifle, and Trial Docket

The March 10, 1893, *Independence Star and Kansan* made this report of Emmett's trial.

Wednesday afternoon strong influences were brought to bear on Emmett to induce him to plead guilty. Although strenuously insisting that he killed nobody during the fight at Coffeyville, he had before expressed a willingness to plead guilty to manslaughter. This the court would not have accepted; but he was given

> to understand that a plea of murder in the
> second degree would be considered. His
> eldest brother, Ben, a man who has always
> been an honorable upright citizen, was
> here and urged him to make that plea. He
> held out for some time but finally yielded.
>
> ... When he pleaded "guilty of murder
> in the second degree" Judge McCue
> proceeded at once to pass sentence,
> making his remarks to the culprit very
> brief and imposing the greatest possible
> penalty. (Samuelson *Story* 149)

Emmett's sentence was imprisonment at hard labor for the rest of his natural life (*Trial Docket*).

The March 10, 1983, *Journal* made only two brief mentions of the trial. The first revealed that Emmett cried like a baby when he heard his sentence. "He claimed that the sentence was unjust, that he was not guilty of murder and had only pleaded guilty to save his friends the expense of fighting the case" ("It is said..."). The second mention follows:

> Emmet [sic] Dalton, the murderer and
> highwayman was sentenced to prison for
> life Wednesday morning by the District
> court at Independence, after a plea of
> guilty had been entered. He was
> immediately placed on a Mo. Pac train,
> with a strong guard conveyed to the
> Penitentiary as fast as steam could carry
> him. ("Emmet Dalton")

The March 10, 1893, *Star and Kansan* reported that Emmett distributed his possessions before he left. Among other bequests he gave his Winchester to Sheriff

Callahan and his pistols to Attorney Fritch (Samuelson *Story* 128).

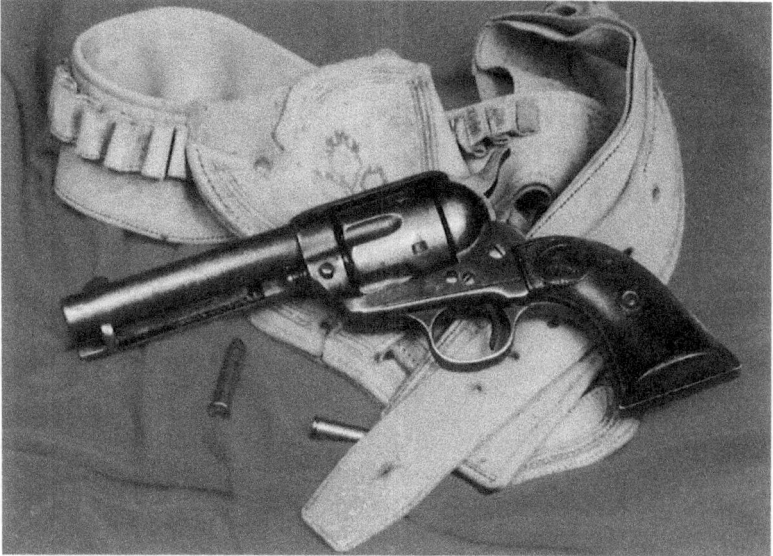

Figure 8.14. Emmett's Six-Shooter with Warrant and Cartridge Belt

Figure 8.15. Bill Power's Revolver

The interest of the outside world did not seem to abate with Emmett's conviction and imprisonment. Artist C. G. Glass continued to sell his photographs of the Daltons and of scenes incident to the raid ("C. G. Glass").

The Commercial Club of Kansas City chartered a special train for an April excursion to Coffeyville. They were met at the depot with a band, greeted by John Kloehr and others, and then given a drive through the town. Each driver told and retold the story of the raid. Bob Dalton's horse, with Bob's rifle strapped to the saddle, was ridden in the parade. Emmett's six-shooters and Grat's Winchester were on display in the Condon windows. Bullet holes remaining from the raid were visible there and in various other locations in the downtown area. Thomas Ayres, whose facial scars were an ever-present reminder of the raid, helped to entertain the Kansas City visitors ("Coffeyville: As Seen").

Figure 8.16. Bullet Holes in Condon Windows.

Figure 8.17. Cartridge Belt showing Damaged
Cartridge: Misshapen after being struck by gunfire from
Coffeyville citizens, this bullet shielded Emmett from at
least one additional wound

With Grant and Bob dead and Emmett in prison for life, their brother Bill Dalton became the fourth outlaw of the family. At some point after Emmett's trial, Bill teamed up with the Bill Doolin gang. Less than two years after his brothers' raid on Coffeyville—on June 8, 1894—Bill was killed by U.S. marshals near Ardmore, Indian Territory. His body was sent to California for burial (Samuelson *Family* 2).

Emmett got along well in prison, working much of the time as a tailor. His mother, who visited him at least twice a year, and C. M. Beeson, a legislator from Ford County, worked to get him paroled. Emmett's arm wound eventually got worse, so in July 1907 he was given a four month parole for medical treatment in

Topeka. When Emmett returned to prison from Topeka on November 1, Kansas Governor Hoch pardoned him.

Fifteen years had passed since the Dalton raid on Coffeyville. Now Emmett was free once more (Samuelson *Story* 150-51). Relatives of the defenders killed and representatives of the banks robbed, as well as many other citizens, protested Emmett's parole to the governor, but to no avail ("Will Pardon Emmett Dalton").[11]

In pardoning Emmett, Governor Hoch made the following statement:

> Every officer of the institution in which he has been confined for the last fifteen years with whom I have conversed share[d] this opinion and expressed it in the strongest possible language…. Scores of prominent people have come to me voluntarily to speak kind words in his behalf…. His youthfulness at the time this awful offense against society was committed must appeal to everyone familiar with the case and prompt the belief that he be given another chance. (Samuelson *Story* 151)

In 1908 Emmett, now a free man, married Julia Johnson Lewis in Bartlesville, Oklahoma. They lived in Bartlesville for several years, during which Emmett wrote *Beyond the Law*. Then they moved to California (Samuelson *Story* 153-59).

In 1931 Emmett and his wife returned to Coffeyville. One of his purposes in returning was to order a tombstone for his brothers' grave. The only marker up to that time had been a piece of the hitching rail to which the Daltons had tied their horses in Death Alley. While in Coffeyville, Emmett also saw to the repair of his brother Frank's stone ("Emmett Dalton Buys Marker").

During that Coffeyville visit, A. B. Macdonald, a *Kansas City Star* reporter, retraced with Emmett the route taken by the gang thirty-nine years earlier. At Elmwood Cemetery, they visited first Frank's grave, then the graves of Grat, Bob, and Bill Power. Emmett pointed to the graves and said,

> I challenge the world to produce the history of an outlaw who ever got anything out of it except that (pointing to the graves) or else huddled in a prison cell.... The biggest fool on earth is the one who thinks that he can beat the law, that crime can be made to pay. It never paid and never will, and that's the one big lesson of the Coffeyville raid. (Dary 121)

The surviving member of the Dalton gang died on July 13, 1937, in California. Emmett's body was cremated. The ashes of the last of the Dalton gang were returned to Oklahoma and scattered over the Dalton plot in the Kingfisher, Oklahoma, cemetery.

Notes to Chapter 8: The Aftermath

1   Elliott used the plural *revolvers* here, but Bob had only one revolver belted on. The two holsters in the Dalton museum (which were gathered from the dead outlaws) each held only one gun. Elliott was probably just emphasizing the point that none of the three revolvers Bob was carrying had been fired.

2   Elliott wrote that the smoke coming from the muzzle of Emmett's rifle "showed that it had been very recently used" (*Last Raid* 58). The October 7th newspaper account does not mention the smoking rifle. This point is interesting, as Emmett later claimed that he did not fire a shot during the raid. We'll never know for certain, but it seems highly unlikely that he fired

it during the last few minutes of the fight. Accounts agreed that he was carrying the sack with the money plus his rifle when he managed to climb on his horse. Then he rode back to Bob and reached down to help him. Emmett would have needed an extra arm if he were also to be firing his rifle during that brief period.

3   Bert Ullom, twenty at the time of the raid, lived in the Farmer's Home with his parents, who were the proprietors of the boarding house. In a 1928 newspaper article, Ullom denied that Emmett was taken to the Farmers' Home, which he said was at the corner of Eighth and Walnut. He claimed that Emmett was taken to the Upham building, which stood then on "the site of the present Traction building" ("Bert Ullom").

The obituary of Ullom's mother, who died in 1937, said the Farmers' Home was "at the intersection of the alley at the 100 block on West Eighth street, the present location of the Traction building" ("Mrs. Tacy Ullom").

I have not been able to establish more definitely the location of the boarding house. I chose to use the alley location in the map because it was closer to the scene of the action and because it seems logical that a man would have to be from close by in order to arrive so quickly with a rope.

4   Marshal Ransome Payne furnished most of the material for *The Dalton Brothers by An Eyewitness*, which became available in late 1892. In that book Payne was credited with capturing Charley Bryant and turning him over to Deputy Short. He also was pictured as "the hero who had trailed them for years and finally run them to the earth" ("The following dispatch..."). Marshal William Grimes and others in authority were incensed at the undeserved credit Payne was taking for himself. A January 5, 1898, letter from Grimes to Payne was published in the *Journal*. In it Grimes said,

> To my knowledge, you never saw Charley Bryant. You were not directly or indirectly instrumental in his capture.... You well know that you never made a step alone to capture the Daltons, and what was credited to you is due to the people of Coffeyville and to those who went down in the fight against the lawless band... you who never did a thing except to go up to Coffeyville and get their pictures after they were dead, and trying [sic] to get their bodies and take them to

California for the reward.... For these and various other reasons..., your commission stands revoked.... ("Grimes to Payne")

5   The October 6th court transcript which included the complaint against Emmett is interesting not only because of the charge but also because of the writing style.

> ... that on the 5th day of Oct 1892 Emit [sic] Dalton did then and there unlawfully feloniously purposely deliberately and premeditatedly wrongfully feloniously and of his malice aforethought assault with a deadly weapon to wit a Winchester repeating rifle loaded with gunpowder and leaden balls which said Winchester repeating rifle so loaded as aforesaid he the said Emit Dalton then and there held in his right hand and which said Winchester repeating rifle loaded as aforesaid he the said Emit Dalton did then and there unlawfully wrongfully purposely maliciously and of his deliberately premeditated malice aforethought fire off and discharge at against and upon the body of him the said Lucius Baldwin thereby and by means thereof striking the said Lucius Baldwin with one of the said leaden balls which leaden ball by force of the Gunpowder aforesaid did penetrate into and through the body of him the said Lucius Baldwin inflicting on and in the body of the said Lucius Baldwin aforesaid one Mortal wound of which mortal wound so inflicted as aforesaid he the said Lucius Baldwin immediately died and so said Emit Dalton by the means acted in the manner aforesaid unlawfully willfully purposely maliciously feloniously and of his deliberately premeditated malice aforethought him the said Lucius Baldwin did then and there kill and murder contrary to the statute in such cases made and provided and against the Peace and dignity of the state of Kansas. (*Case File #7257*)

6   Actually Adeline, Ben, Bill (often called Will in the newspapers, including the October 7th account), Simon, and Eva all came to Coffeyville (Samuelson *Story* 118).

7   Samuelson notes that additional letters to the *Kansas City Journal* verified that the congressman was quoted correctly (*Story* 121).

8   The transcript at one point charged Emmett with the murder committed during the robbery of the First National Bank of Independence.

9   After all the furor over the guns and over the remarks made by papers critical of the *Journal* and its editor, Elliott had evidently decided to avoid mentioning Emmett Dalton except in the briefest way possible. The *Journal* did not report directly on Dalton's December appearance in court but reprinted an article about it from the December 23rd *Independence Star and Kansan*. That article reported that on December 19th Emmett had been taken to district court where he was ordered to be ready for trial the next week ("Emmet [sic] Dalton"). The *Star and Kansan* report was incorrect; records showed that Emmett appeared on December 14th and 16th and that his hearing was set for January.

10 Again Editor Elliott gave minimal space to what was surely big news. Many Coffeyville citizens traveled to Independence to be present for the January 16th hearing. The *Journal* only reported that on January 16, 1893, Emmett appeared before Judge Gilmore in Independence charged with killing George Cubine. He was bound over without bail for the March term of court ("Bound Over").

11 A letter reportedly written by Emmett to his mother in an attempt to prevent the raid on Coffeyville may have influenced Hoch. Though Emmett's parole seems justified both by the details of his trial and his good conduct in prison, I consider the letter highly suspect, mainly because of its timing. If Emmett had really written it before the Coffeyville raid, the letter would have been helpful at his trial. Why did the letter only appear after he'd served fifteen years of his life term? Because Governor Hoch was then trying to decide whether or not to pardon Emmett, the timing of the new "evidence" presented by the letter seems certainly fortuitous.

Finally, since Bill knew enough about legalities to succeed in getting Emmett's horse and guns and Bob's $900 returned, it seems likely he would have seen to it that the letter was presented at Emmett's trial, had it existed at that time. Here is the text of the letter as it appeared in the April 17, 1908, *Oklahoma City Times*:

_____, Ind. Ter., October 1, 1892. Dear Mother: Get somebody to see Bob at once. He has planned to rob two banks in _____ on the 5th. Am with him now, but he will not listen to me. If he pulls off this job, I will have to go with him. Grat is in it too, and I won't let them think I am a quitter, so will go with them, unless somebody talks them out of it. It's going to be close to where we used to live. If Will is in Kingfisher, send him. He knows where we are. Yours. Em. (Samuelson *Story* 152-53)

Afterword

Though the Daltons were notorious before their October 1892 raid on Coffeyville's two banks, they had not yet killed anyone in the course of their outlaw career. That Wednesday morning raid changed everything. Besides bringing death or injury to seven Coffeyville citizens, the raid brought death to Grat Dalton, Bob Dalton, Bill Power, and Dick Broadwell, and painful wounds and a jail term to Emmett Dalton.

Their train-robbing days may have seemed like a lark to the young men. If they had continued as train robbers, the end of their story might have been very different. But the Daltons didn't stay with trains; they progressed to banks.

The Dalton raid on Coffeyville's two banks was ill-conceived and poorly planned. The three outlaws in the Condon allowed themselves to be outsmarted by a simple ruse. The townspeople thus had time to arm themselves. Though some shots had been fired by the time Bob and Emmett went out the back door of the First National Bank, the situation was not yet out of control. No one had been wounded. One might speculate that, had Bob not shot Lucius Baldwin, the gang might have been arrested without serious injury to anyone.

But Bob did shoot and kill Lucius Baldwin. That act was the catalyst that precipitated the gunfight. Since Bob himself did not outlive the raid, no one had a chance to ask him whether that shot was deliberately aimed or was just an unlucky fluke, unlucky for Lucius Baldwin, but also unlucky for many others both on and off the Coffeyville plaza that day.

Knowing he had, at the very least, seriously injured one man, Bob might have decided he and the rest of the gang were now in such serious trouble that more shootings wouldn't matter. He certainly fired with deadly accuracy when he and Emmett crossed Union. Only during the trial did witnesses suggest that Emmett might have killed Cubine. Earlier reports credited Bob's deadly aim. Before being wounded himself, Bob probably was responsible not only for the death of Lucius Baldwin but also for the deaths of George Cubine and Charles Brown and the wounding of Charles Gump, Thomas Ayres, and Arthur Reynolds.

Grat Dalton was responsible for Marshal Connelly's death—shooting him in the back. By the time of that shooting, however, Grat and his two cohorts from the Condon had been under heavy fire. All three had all been wounded. Grat might have still hoped escape was possible when he saw the Marshal step into the alley and stand between him and the tethered Dalton horses.

Because Coffeyville wished to honor the citizens who died during the Dalton Raid, the Dalton Defenders Museum and Dalton Defenders Days were named in their honor. Baldwin, Cubine, Brown, and Connelly—these names may not be so well known as those of the outlaws, but the four Coffeyville citizens also deserve a special kind of posthumous fame. Each of them died with a gun in his hand, a gun he had taken up in order to uphold the law and defend the property of his townsmen. John Kloehr wrote, "the world likes a man who does his duty well." Those men were seeking to do their duty well in an emergency. They rose to the occasion.

Though one hundred years have passed since that day in October of 1892, let us hope that the example of the Dalton Defenders continues to instill the citizens of Coffeyville both with respect for the lessons of the past and with the willingness to do what must be done.

The events of the Dalton Raid and Death Alley have lent a flavor of the Old West to the town of Coffeyville. And that flavor is one that venerates courage, individuality, independence, and self-reliance—all qualities much in evidence in Coffeyville, Kansas, on October 5, 1892. A paraphrase of the message on John Kloehr's medal seems appropriate: the emergency arose, and the men appeared.

Bibliography

Adams, Ramon F. *Burs Under the Saddle: A Second Look at Books and Histories of the West*. Norman, OK: University of OK Press, 1964.

_____. *Six-Guns and Saddle Leather: A Bibliography of Books and Pamphlets on Western Outlaws and Gunmen*. Norman, OK: University of OK Press, 1969.

Arnold, Anna E. *A History of Kansas*. Topeka, KS: KS Printer, 1931.

"Bert Ullom Makes First Visit Since He Left Here in 1892." *Coffeyville Journal* 28 July 1928: 11.

"Bound Over." *The Journal* 20 January 1893: 5.

Branson, Branley Allan and Mary Louise Branson. "At Coffeyville, the Dalton Museum Recalls the West's Most Ambitious Holdup." *Wild West* February 1991: 62, 64, 69-72, 74.

Breihan, Carl W. *Lawmen and Robbers*. Caldwell, ID: Caxton Printers, 1986: 20-29.

"A Card." *The Journal* 14 October 1892: 4.

Carpenter, Charles T. [The Carpenter Story (circa 1938)] *Coffeyville, KS at 100: 1869-1969: History and Centennial Celebration*. Coffeyville, KS: Coffeyville Journal Press, 1969: 24-26.

Case File #7257: Montgomery County District Court. Independence, KS: State of Kansas, 17 November 1892.

Case File #7287: Montgomery County District Court. Independence, KS: State of Kansas, 13 January 1893.

"C. G. Glass." *The Journal* 6 January 1893: 7.

"Citizens Meet and Take Action." *The Journal* 7 October 1892: 5.

"Coffeyville: As Seen by Our Kansas City Visitors." *The Journal* 21 April 1893: 1.

Coffeyville, KS at 100: 1869-1969: History and Centennial Celebration. Coffeyville, KS: Coffeyville Journal Press, 1969: 20-27.

Craven, Glen. "Descendant of Emmett Blasts Myths." *Coffeyville Journal* 2 October 1991: 11-12.

The Dalton Brothers and Their Astounding Career of Crime: By an Eye Witness. 1892. Introduction by Burton Rascoe. New York: Frederick Fell, Inc.: 1954.

Dalton, Emmett. *Beyond the Law.* 1918. Coffeyville, KS: Coffeyville Historical Society, n.d.

_____. *When the Daltons Rode.* Garden City, NY: Sun Dial Press, 1937.

"Dalton Raid: Praise for Coffeyville." *The Journal* 14 October 1892: 4.

"Daltons! Gang Meets Doom: Tales Differ on Sequences." *Coffeyville Journal* 1 October 1980: 1D-2D.

Dary, David. *True Tales of Old-Time Kansas.* Lawrence, KS: University Press of Kansas, 1984: 114-24.

Duncan, L. Wallace. *History of Montgomery County, Kansas: By Its Own People.* Iola, KS: Press of Iola Register, 1903: 33-41.

Elliott, David Stewart. "Daltons! The Robber Gang Meet their Waterloo in Coffeyville." *The Journal* 7 October 1892: 5-6.

_____. *Last Raid of the Daltons: Battle with the Bandits at Coffeyville, KS, October 5, 1892.* 1892. Coffeyville, KS: Coffeyville Journal Print, 1954.

"Emmet Dalton [sic]." *The Journal* 3 March 1893: 9.

"Emmett Dalton Buys Marker for Graves of Slain Brothers." *Coffeyville Journal* 1 May 1931: 3.

"Family Prompted Narrative: Copies Given to Step-Children." *Coffeyville Journal* 1 October 1980: 3D.

"The following dispatch ..." *The Journal* 3 February 1893: 1.

Graves, Richard S. *Oklahoma Outlaws: A Graphic History of the Early Days in Oklahoma; the Bandits who Terrorized the First Settlers and the Marshals who Fought them to Extinction; Covering a Period of Twenty-five Years.* Fort Davis, TX: Frontier Book Co., 1968.

Green, Fritz. "Relative of Lucius Baldwin Keeps Historic Letters." *Coffeyville Journal* 2 October 1991: 10.

"Grimes to Payne." *The Journal* 17 February 1893: 2.

Horan, James D. *The Authentic Wild West: The Outlaws.* New York: Crown Publishers, 1977: 146-64, 298.

Howes, Charles C. *This Place Called Kansas.* Norman, OK: University of Oklahoma Press, 1984.

Huff, Roger. "100 Years Ago: Daltons' Crime Spree." *Coffeyville Journal* 2 October 1991: 5.

_____. "Movies Put Action Above Fact in Dalton Story." *Coffeyville Journal* 2 October 1991: 13.

"A Human Hyena." *The Journal* 9 December 1892: 4.

"In Memoriam [Connelly]. *The Journal* 7 October 1892: 5.

"In Memoriam [Cubine]." *The Journal* 14 October 1892: 4.

"It is said ..." *The Journal* 10 March 1893: 11.

"John J. Kloehr of Dalton Fame Dies." *Coffeyville Journal* 21 March 1927: 1-2.

Kloehr, John J. Letter to Holmes Hodge. In *The Journal* 4 November 1892: 6.

Latta, Frank F. *Dalton Gang Days*. Santa Cruz, CA: Bear State Books, 1976.

Map of Coffeeville [sic] Montgomery Co Kansas. New York: Sanborn-Perris Map Co., Ltd, 1890.

McKennon, C.H. "The Last Raid of the Dalton Gang [from circa 1964 interview with W. C. Stamper]." *Tulsa Sunday World* 7 July 1974: 12-13.

McLoughlin, Denis. *Wild and Woolly: Encyclopedia of the Old West*. New York, NY: Doubleday, 1975: 124-27, 252-54, 559-60.

McNeal, T. A. *When Kansas Was Young*. New York: Macmillan, 1922: 271-76.

"More Robbers!" *The Journal* 14 October 1892: 4.

"Mrs. Tacy Ullom Dies at Elkhart." *Coffeyville Daily Journal* 19 October 1937: 3.

Nash, Jay Robert. *Bloodletters and Badmen: A Narrative Encyclopedia of American Criminals from the Pilgrims to the Present*. New York, NY: Evans and Co., 1973: 145-49.

"Obituary [Brown]." *The Journal* 14 October 1892: 4.

"Obituary of Lucius M. Baldwin." *The Journal* 21 October 1892: 4.

"Our Friends, the Enemy." *The Journal* 9 December 1892: 6.

Pannill, Mark S. *The Sixth Man; Who was She?* Waxahachie, TX: VinCon Publishing, 1987.

Perry, Jacob Thomas. "Witness Recounts Robbery: Watched Shooting from Store: Account Written in 1957." *Coffeyville Journal* 1 October 1980: 1D-3D.

Pippenger, Gretchen. "Fictional Novel Written." *Coffeyville Journal* 2 October 1991: 14.

Preece, Harold. *The Dalton Gang: End of an Outlaw Era*. New York, NY: Hastings House Publishers, 1963.

"Read's Began as Trading Post." *Coffeyville Journal* 1 October 1980: 6D.

"Relief Committee Meeting." *The Journal* 2 December 1892: 6.

"Reprint of Col. Elliott's Dalton Book is Off Press." *Coffeyville Journal* 12 July 1954: n.p.

Samuelson, Nancy B. *The Dalton Gang Family: A Genealogical Study of the Dalton Outlaws and their Family Connections.* Meade, KS; Back Room Printing, 1989.

——————————. *The Dalton Gang Story: Lawmen to Outlaws.* Eastford, CT: Shooting Star Press, 1992.

Steele, Philip W. *In Search of the Daltons.* Springdale, AK: Frontier Press, 1985.

Tibbils, W. H. Letter to D. Stewart Elliott. *The Journal* 21 October 1892: 4.

"Tid-Bits from the Telegram." *The Journal* 4 November 1892: 6.

"Too Excited to Be Scared by Daltons." *Coffeyville Journal* 22 February 1952: n.p.

Trial Docket: March Term. Independence, KS: Montgomery County, 1893.

"Will Pardon Emmett Dalton." *Coffeyville Journal* 25 October 1907: 1.

"Working Their Scheme." *The Journal* 2 December 1892: 6.